Customizing Your Computer

Inside the *Control Panel* you will find tools that customize and help configure your computer.

On the next few page  w of the tools to help yo) it looks and works the v ng:

◊ Changing ho
◊ How to install a printer.
◊ How to use Add/Remove Programs

To Enter the Control Panel:

◊**With XP**: Start > Settings > Control Panel

◊**With Vista**: Start > Control Panel

◊**With Windows 7**: Start > Control Panel

My Computer, My Way! Yeah!

Control Panel

It's important to have a look in your Control Panel.

Some things in the Control Panel you don't want to mess with unless you know what you're doing. But other things, like setting up how your desktop looks, personalizing your mouse, setting up devices like printers... these are things you'll want to personalize.

Your Control Panel might not look the same as what I show on the next page. It might have a different layout.

To change the layout, look on the right side of the window for *View by* and click on the arrow. Then make your selection.

With Windows 7, you can choose to view by:

◊ Category
◊ Large icons
◊ Small icons.

If you choose the Icon View, everything is listed individually. Nothing is buried in a category!

With XP, the Control Panel views are called:

◊ Category View, much like I'm showing
◊ Classic View, where everything is listed.

Control Panel - Windows 7

Within the Control Panel you can adjust or customize many things. Here are just a few:

◊ Customize your Desktop.

◊ Adjust your Keyboard settings.

◊ Set the Parental Controls.

◊ Program scheduled tasks, such as defragging!

◊ Set your Power Saving options.

◊ Set how your mouse works.

◊ Adjust the date and time—even the time zone!

Customize your mouse!

Are you a lefty? Is your
mouse a righty?

You can customize your
mouse so the left and right
clickers work just right for you!

Here's the path you click to open this tool:

If you`re viewing the Control Panel by Category...
Start > Control Panel > Appearance & Personalization
> Change the theme > Change mouse pointers

I know, it's a weird place to find it!
Here's an easier way.

View the Control Panel by icons in Windows 7, Vista or
Classic view in XP. Then the path is:

Start > Control Panel > Mouse

A window will open up with lots of options, including:

◊   How the buttons on your mouse work.

◊   How the pointer looks on your screen.

◊   How fast the mouse pointer travels.

NOTE - IN THIS GUIDE,
When I say left-click or right-click:
Left click gives commands, and
Right click gets commands
(opens the mouse menu).

Desktop

What's a Desktop?
The desktop is what your monitor looks like when you don't have any programs running.
You can personalize it with your own pictures, change the size of the icons, change your screen saver...

There are two ways to open the window to personalize your desktop.

One way is to go through the Start menu:

With XP
Start > Settings > Control Panel > Display Properties

With Vista and 7
Start > Control Panel > Appearance & Personalize

Or the easy way!

Right click anywhere on your desktop, then:
with XP, click on Properties
with Vista or 7, click on Personalize

You can pick and choose the settings by ticking or unticking, the things you want to change.

Desktop - with XP

When you click on Display Properties you will open a window with five tabs: Themes, Desktop, Screen Saver, Appearance and Settings.

Themes are the "full meal deal" settings in Display Properties. Choose a Theme to set the overall look of your desktop: the background, screen saver, font size, colors, how your mouse pointer looks, even sounds!

You can customize any part of a theme by clicking on the other tabs and choosing the options you want!

Tip
    If you see a picture you would like for your
    desktop background, all you have to do is right
    click over it and choose Set as Background!

Desktop, What's what

Screen Savers

Screen savers originated to prevent *ghosting,* which happened with early-technology monitors. Ghosting is almost non-existent with current technology, so today's screen savers are mostly decorative and entertaining.

Screen savers can also offer a certain level of privacy, if you require a password to re-open your system once the screen saver is active.

Appearance

Have a look at the color and font (style of typing) in the Task Bar (beside the Start menu button) or along the Title Bar at the top. You can change the color and the font style of the print to almost anything you want!

Screen Resolution in Settings

Screen resolution refers to the number of pixels on the screen. 1024 x 768 means there are 1024 pixels across, and 768 down. This gives you a good picture on a 15-inch monitor. A higher resolution will give you a more detailed image.

Pixels - A pixel is a dot. The display on your screen is made of up these dots (pixels).This picture has VERY large pixels! Can you guess who it is?

Desktop - 7 & Vista

Personalizing your desktop with Vista and Windows 7 is simple!

Open up your Control Panel, click on PERSONALIZATION.

A window similar to this one will open.

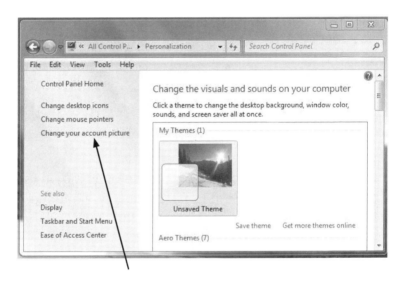

Click on what you would like to change from the list on the left.

Taskbar and StartMenu
The Taskbar is the bar that shows along the bottom of your screen. It shows some "quick launch" icons for a few programs, as well as any programs you have open.

Devices & Printers

A device is anything that is attached to your computer: your printer, a camera, a fax machine, speakers, a mouse...

To find your printer or device settings

In XP: Start > Printers & Faxes
In Vista & 7: Start > Devices & Printers

Installing devices, most times, 😊 will mean no more than putting in its installation disk and attaching it to the right port in your computer.

Each device attached to your computer is *driven by a Driver,* including your printer. You don't really have to know much about drivers, but a wee bit of knowledge here helps things make more sense.

Here's the skinny on Drivers!
The operating system in your computer works in a very generic language. Remember about protocols that the internet uses? This is the same kind of thing.

But, every device speaks in its own secret language, I guess to protect brand technology. So, between the device and your computer, a translator so-to-speak, is needed. *Hence the Driver.*

Bonjour = Hello
Hello = Bonjour

The Driver for a device will be on its installation disk. If you do not have an installation disk you might have to download a driver from the maker's web site.

Devices & Printers

Installing & Troubleshooting Devices

Here's how to install a printer:

1. First open the printer and/or device window. (Start > Devices & Printers)

2. This window will also show if you have any printers or devices already installed. If you want to install something new, look for and click on *Add a Printer or Device*, seen on the side or top of this window.

If you already have a printer or device installed, it will show up here. If it's active, it will have a √ check mark beside it. If it doesn't, right click over it and choose - Make Active!

If you're adding (installing) a printer, click on "Add a printer" and follow along with the prompts.

Here's how to Troubleshoot

◊ With XP, click on Printer>Properties. You will see an option to "Print a test page". Try that. If it doesn't work, your program will then try and help you fix it, by walking you through its *trouble shooting* steps.

◊ With Vista & 7, right click over its icon in the Device window and choose Troubleshoot. Follow along with the steps!

Good luck!

Add/Remove Programs

When we first got a computer, Pat, our computer guru, couldn't stress to us enough that when it came to **removing programs,** to *use this feature.* Over the years I have come to understand why.

You can easily delete a program simply by right-clicking on its name, found through the start menu. But if you delete this way, you'll only delete what you see, and leave crumbs of it all around in your system.

Using *Add/Remove Programs* is like having Super-maid help with the housework. Every little part of the program gets picked up, cleaned out and removed, even the crumbs!

Here's where to find it:

◊ XP: Settings > Control Panel > Add/Remove Program

◊ Vista: Control Panel > Programs > Uninstall a Program

◊ Windows 7: Control Panel > Programs and Features > Uninstall or Change a Program

A window will open that displays a list of all the programs that are installed in your computer. If you click over the name of a program, you will see options to Repair, Change or Remove it.

Choose what you want and *just do it!*

General Maintenance

A little regular maintenance will help your computer run smoothly. These tools are easy to start, and they do all the work by themselves! **You** just have to remember to use them!

If you notice your computer is running slowly, running Disk Cleanup and Disk Defragmenter might help fix the problem. You can even schedule them to work on their own!

Here's how to find them with Windows 7:

Microsoft got it right with Windows 7.
To find any of these tools, all you have to do is:

1. Type what you're looking for in the Search Window. (It's right above the start button)

   ◊   Type in Disk and you'll see both the Clean-up and Defrag tools.

   ◊   Type in Schedule to find Scheduled tasks

You can also find these tools in the Control Panel under System & Security > Administrative tools.
         But using the Search window is the way to go!

Disk Cleanup

What is it for?

Disk Cleanup can help free up space and clutter on your hard drive by removing things like temporary internet files, cookies and emptying your trash.

After you run Disk Cleanup, it will ask if *you are sure you want to delete these items*. You can view them if you want. I usually say *Yes,* and never regret it.

Here's how to find it with XP & Vista:

1. Start > Programs > Accessories > System Tools > Disk Cleanup

2. Choose where in your computer you want Disk Cleanup to work.
   - ◊ In XP, it asks you which drive to clean up. The "C" drive is your main drive and the most important to do.
   - ◊ With Vista, you're asked "my files only" or all the files. *(While you're at it, it doesn't hurt to clean the whole house!)*

3. When the job is complete a report will pop up showing you the results.

4. You can choose to view the files it suggests you delete, or just click OK and be done with them.

> TIP:
> System Tools will run faster if all other programs are turned off.

Disk Defrag

The Disk Defragmenter!

Just like *Mr. Spock,* computers want things in a logical order. The Disk Defragmenter helps to keep files organized by picking up fragments of data that are misfiled, and putting them where they belong.

Here's how to find it with XP & Vista:

1. Start > Programs > Accessories > System Tools > Disk Defragmenter

2. Click *Defragment*

> Yep, that's it.

Something to know about the defragging:
it might not be quick!
The messier your computer,
the longer it's going to take...

Remember, System Tools works faster if you are not running any other programs.

Scheduled Tasks

Scheduled Tasks

This little wizard can help you set up a regular maintenance program. *Scheduled Tasks* can also get your computer to do a bunch of jobs automatically, even check for email!

Open it to see a whole list of programs. It will ask you what programs you want to run and when.

Here's how to find it with XP & Vista:

1. Start > Programs > Accessories > System Tools > Scheduled Tasks (in Vista it's called Task Scheduler)

2. A *Wizard* window will pop up asking you what programs you would like to run.

3. Follow the directions, step-by-step, with the help of the *Wizard.*

4. Click Finish when you're done.

Tip:
For Scheduled Tasks to work, your computer must be on during the times you have told it to run!

Deleting Files

You've probably discovered that it is easy to create files by mistake — I know I have. Don't worry though, it's easy to delete unwanted files or folders.

Here's how with XP and Vista

OPEN		
Look-In	MY DOCUMENTS	various icons
Folders inside the main folder will look open or closed. If open you will see the names of the files inside!	Highlight The File you want by ↓ clicking over it!	
File Name	The File	OPEN
Files of Type		CANCEL

With Vista and XP, open a folder like My Documents or My Pictures and delete directly from there.

1. Open the folder you think your file is in. For instance, click: Start > My Documents

A window will open with the names of files listed.

3. Left click your mouse over the file you want to delete to select it.

4. **Right-click, to open a mouse menu then left click on Delete!**

Select
Open
Print
Copy
Create Shortcut
Delete
Rename
Properties

Deleting Files

Here's how with Windows 7

Windows 7 organizes files beautifully in "Libraries", making it much easier to find files!

Down on your Taskbar, click on and open Windows Explorer by clicking on the Windows Explorer icon. (not to be confused with the Internet Explorer icon...) It looks like a file folder.

See Libraries in the left column, and your folders listed under it? Documents, Pictures, etc. Click on a folder to view its contents. You can view the files as a list or like I show here, as large thumbnails!

Right click over a file to open a mouse menu. Slide your mouse to Delete and left click. Gone!

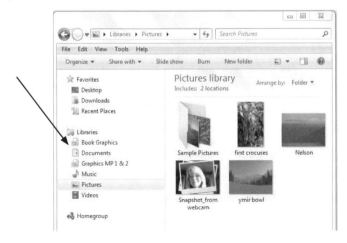

Trash & Recycling

Your computer has a Trash Can and/or a Recycling Bin. When you delete a file or folder, it goes directly there.

Where?
You should have an icon on your desktop for your trash or recycling. Left click on the icon to open it.

When your Trash/Recycling folder is open, it will show all the files and folders that you have deleted since the last time it was emptied. This is a good thing, because if you deleted something by mistake, at this point it's easy to get it back.

Notice the options in the left sidebar:

◊   Empty Recycle Bin

◊   Restore all items

If you highlight a single file,
"Restore all items"
will change to
"Restore item"

The Recycling Bin is your safety net!

Trash & Recycling

To Retrieve from the Recycle Bin

1. Open the Recycle bin.

2. Highlight the file you want to retrieve.

3. Right-click and choose *Restore,* or move your mouse to the *Restore item* option in the left sidebar.

It is important to
Empty the Recycle Bin!

When you are sure that there is NOTHING in the Recycle bin that you want to retrieve, empty it.

Here's how to Empty the Recycle bin:
1. Open the Recycle bin
2. In the left sidebar, click on *Empty Recycle Bin.*

Once you have emptied the Recycle Bin, files are gone forever... *unless you are a tech wizard!*

Tip:
Did you accidentally delete your recycle bin from your desktop?
Right-click anywhere on your desktop to open a mouse menu, click on "Personalize" and then desktop icons.
You'll be able to reset it from there!

Windows Explorer

There is a very cool program in your computer called **Windows Explorer**.

With Windows Explorer you can see all the files and all the folders in your computer, making it **very easy** to find, move or delete any file. Really!

Microsoft finally got how great Windows Explorer is with Windows 7! The layout is a little better than it was before and now you can even open Windows Explorer directly from an icon on the taskbar.

Folders 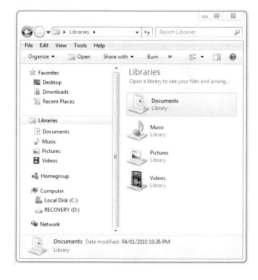 Sub-folders & Files

The Windows 7 Explorer window

Windows Explorer

You can view the files a bunch of different ways, by clicking on the views icon.
Use the slider to change the view

Try it out, it's pretty cool. With Extra Large Icons, you can practically read a document. Details will show you what type of file it is and when the file was last modified.

> Click over a folder on the left side
> and see its contents in the right side.

With Vista and XP,
find Windows Explorer this way:

In Vista:
◊   Start > Programs > Windows Explorer

In XP:
◊   Start > Programs > Accessories > Windows Explorer

Windows Explorer

On this side of Windows Explorer you will see the different drives in your computer and folders that contain programs and documents.	Click on a folder on the left side and you will see its contents on this side! Here, "My Documents" is open, showing the folders and files inside. Highlight a file on this side to delete or move it.
▤ Desktop	▤ Basketball
▤ My Computer	▤ My Book Drafts
▤ My Network	▤ School Stuff
▤ My Documents	📄 First Save
🗑 Recycle Bin	📄 Second Save

To delete a file or folder in Windows Explorer:
Be careful not to delete files or folders
that are essential to your computer!
Only delete your own stuff.

1. **Left click** on a file or folder to highlight it.

2. **Right click** to open the mouse menu then choose Delete. **Left click** to give the command.

Select
Open
Print
Copy
Create Shortcut
Delete
Rename
Properties

3. It will ask you if you really want to delete this. Click *Yes* if you do, *No* if you don't!

Windows Explorer

To move a file or folder it's just

CLICK & DRAG!

This is too easy to be true!

1. Click through the folders shown in **the left side window** until the file you are looking for shows up in the **right-side window**.

2. Now, back **in the left-side window**, scroll around, up and down, until you can **see the folder** you want the file <u>moved to</u>. As long as you don't click on anything, the right side window will stay the same!

3. In the right-side window, left-click on the file you're going to move to highlight it. **CAPTURE it, by holding the left-click down. Now, with the mouse still clicked down, simply drag the file** directly to, and over, the name of the folder you want to deposit it in.

4. Release your mouse. That's it—Moved!

If only moving day was this easy....

Tip
If you accidentally drop the file into the wrong folder, just click
"Edit > Undo"
and try again!

Games

This doesn't have anything to do with customizing your computer, but it's important to remember to play.

Don't forget, you can just have fun with your computer too! Lucky for us, most computers come with a few games pre-installed!

Some of the more common games are Solitaire, Hearts, Pinball and Backgammon. You might also see internet games! These are all really fun to play and you don't have to give any personal information to play them. Just click to open and follow a couple of prompts. It's that easy!

Here's how to find them:

1. Start > Programs > Games
   or with 7, Start > Games
2. Click on the game you want to open.
3. PLAY!

REVVING UP YOUR DOCUMENTS!

A couple little tricks here and there can really make a difference when it comes to using your computer.

The next few pages will show you how easy it is to fancy up your documents.

REVVING UP YOUR DOCUMENTS!

Changing Default Font

If you don't like the size or style of typing that appears every time you open your word processing program you can **change the default setting** to almost anything you like!

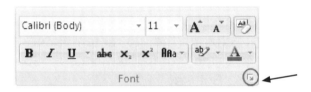

Here`s how with Word 07

1. Click on the Home Tab, then the little dialog launcher at the bottom of the Font group.

2. A new font window will open. Click on the fonts and styles you want.

3. Click on Default, and then say Yes to your changes!

Here`s how with Microsoft Works:

1. Open a blank document.

2. Change the font options along the menu bar.

3. Click File > Save as, then Template

4. Give the template a name, like My Default font

5. Tick "Use this template for new documents"

6. OK and you're done!

Changing Default Font

Here's how to change the default font in Word 02

1. Open Word and a new blank document

2. To open the font window click: Format > Font

3. Within the font window you can choose the size and style of fonts.

4. Once you have chosen what you want, you **MUST click on the Default button** at the bottom left-hand corner of this window.

5. Word will ask if you are sure you want to do this, as it will **"change the global template."** It might also refer to the "normal" template.   Sounds very ominous… But, say YES!

Now every time you open Word, it will look the way YOU want it to look and that's very nice indeed.

◊ You can change the fonts in your documents any time you like.

◊ You can select text by highlighting it, then choose a new one.

◊ Use the *Select All* tool if you want to change the font in an entire document.

◊ If you don`t like what you`ve done, remember, there is always the Undo tool!

Spelling and Grammar

Spelling and Grammar
This tool checks spelling and grammar automatically
as you type.

To point out mistakes you will see a wavy red
underline to show possible spelling mistakes, and a
wavy green underline, to show possible errors with
your grammar. **These lines do not show up when
you print the document.**

Did you notice I said "possible" mistakes or errors?

Spell check is only as smart as its programmer; they're
pretty smart, but... For instance, Spell Check will think
an unknown name is a mistake, like Latremouille!
Go figure?

When you have typed a word that you know is right,
but your computer doesn't recognize, you have to *Add*
the new word to its dictionary.

Next: how to customize Spelling and Grammar!

Auto Correct Spelling

Customize your AutoCorrect window. Here's how:

In Word 2002 & Works click: Tools > Auto Correct

In Word 2007: Click the Office Button, then Word Options (bottom right side of menu), then Proofing to Auto Correct options!

You will open a window like this one.

1. Type the word you often misspell, *the way you misspell it,* in the **Replace** window.

2. Then, in the **With** window, type in the correct spelling.

Tailored to a perfect fit!

Page Layout

Adjusting the margins on your page is easy to do.

Here`s where to find it:

In Works and Word 02:
File > Page Setup

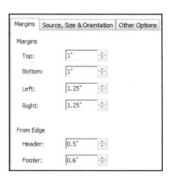

Make any adjustments
by typing directly in the
windows or by clicking on
the arrows.

In Word 07:
Page Layout Tab >
Page Setup group

Click on Margins to
see a variety of margin options or choose custom!

---

8 1/2 x 11 inch paper is called Letter size.

Remember if you change the paper size of your
document, you will have to tell your printer too.

...When you print!

Line Spacing
Find the tools to adjust line spacing within Paragraph.

Word 07: Home Tap > Paragraph

Works & Word 02: Format > Paragraph

Keyboard Shortcuts

Letting go of the keyboard, grabbing the mouse, moving back to your keyboard, doesn't sound like much. But if you have to do it repeatedly, it might drive you nuts! That's why it is nice to know at least a couple of keyboard shortcuts!

Using shortcuts can make a world of difference if you use a command quite often.

Things to know about keyboard shortcuts:

◊ Press the CTRL or ALT key first, then the key you are using for the shortcut.

◊ The keys must be all be depressed at the same time to make the shortcut active.

◊ You can use a shortcut on highlighted material.

◊ You can use a shortcut to change the font of what you will type next.

◊ Use it once to turn it on, use it again to turn it off!

Almost anything you do with your mouse, you can do with a keyboard shortcut!

Keyboard Shortcuts

Here is a list of common shortcuts

◊ CTRL + C   Copy the selected text or graphic

◊ CTRL + V   Pas**te** whatever you just copied!

◊ CTRL + B   Type **bold**

◊ CTRL + I   Type *italic*

◊ CTRL + U   Type <u>underlined</u>

◊ CTRL + X   Erase the selected text or graphic

◊ CTRL + P   Print

◊ CTRL + Z   Undo the last action

◊ CTRL + Y   Redo the last action

◊ CTRL + Shift + **<**   Decrease font size

◊ CTRL + Shift + **>**   Increase font size

Sometimes a shortcut IS a good idea!

Bright Ideas

Letters & Mailings

I'm always learning new things in Word! And the day I finally felt brave enough to try Letters and Mailings was a good one! **Here's how to find it:**

In Word 2002: Tools > Letters & Mailings > ...

In Works: Find what you need under Tools

In Word 2007: Mailings Tab > Mail Merge

Letters & Mailings	**Mail Merge Wizard...**
	Show Mail Merge Toolbar
	Envelopes & Labels
	Letter Wizard

Mail Merge Wizard...

Mail Merge is what companies use to personalize form letters. You can use the Mail Merge Wizard to help you create personalized:

- Letters
- Email Messages
- Envelopes
- Labels
- Directories

"Merge" — a great word that explains a lot!
This function looks for information, maybe a list of addresses or names, from somewhere else in your computer, then puts that information **into** another document!

How cool is that!

Mail Merge

How does Mail Merge work?
Simply put, the programs talk to each other. As always, it's easier to understand after you do it, so...

◊ **Open an Address Book in your computer**
(My address book is part of my email program)

◊ The address book will be your **Data-Source**.

◊ Now, open up someone in your address book, a *Contact*, to see the information (properties) you have for them.

◊ The windows where you see their name, address, phone number, email address, etc., are called fields.

◊ **<<Fields>> This term is important to know.**

◊ The more complete the fields are in your data-source, the more mail merge can do for you.

When you use Mail Merge, you insert various <<fields>> into your letter or document. For example; if I want to send the same letter to 10 people from my address book, parts of the letter on my computer screen might look like this:

Dear <<First>>,

Look at your contact's information. See the field where it says "First"? Word looks for the specified field, then inserts that information into your letter!

Mail Merge

It is not too hard to follow the steps when you use Mail Merge in Word. But you will find the steps easier if you are using a full version of Microsoft Office, which includes the email program, Outlook.

When you use your address book as the data source for Mail Merge, make sure that you have **all** the fields in your address book filled out correctly.

If you are going to try Mail Merge in Works, you will have to export your address book into a data file that Works can use, like .csv (comma separated values).

You deserve a drum roll!
Just because.

Envelopes & Labels

Envelopes and Labels
If you want to print out envelopes or labels you need to tell your printer what size of envelope or label you are using. This tool lets you do just that.

Here`s where to find Envelopes & Labels

◊ **In Works:** Envelopes and Labels are both under Tools

◊ **In Word 2002:** Tools > Letters & Mailings > Envelopes & Labels > Labels tab

◊ **In Word 2007:** Mailings tab, Envelopes and Labels grouped on the left.

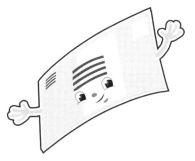

TIP!
Buying a label that is listed in the label "options" (and most are!) makes it easy for your printer to print the information in just the right spot!

Envelopes & Labels

Printing on Envelopes

Open the "Envelope" tab:
◊ Type in the delivery and return addresses in the windows provided.
◊ Click on "Options" and tell it what size of envelope you have.
◊ Put your envelope in the printer and click OK!

Printing on Labels

This is a great feature if you would like to print out labels for canning, wine, CDs, addresses, whatever!

Open the "Labels" tab:
◊ Click on "Options" and choose the type and size of label you're using.

Now you have a couple of choices. You can either type the information in the space provided, and click on Print, and you're done.

Or..... Fancy up your label by...

◊ Type the address, or what you want, in the space provided.

◊ Right click, to open a mouse menu.

◊ Choose Font, to change font or colors.

◊ Choose Paragraph, to change alignment.

◊ Click on Print and you're done!   *Ta Da!*

Letter Templates

Templates are great preformatted professional looking documents, like cover letters, faxes, resumes, brochures, awards....

Everything is all set up. Just click your mouse into the spaces provided and type your own words!

Here's where you find Templates:

◊ **In Works**: File > New, brings you to the Microsoft Works Task Launcher. Click on Templates along the top, and if you like, choose a category from the left side. Click on the template you want!

◊ **In Word 2002:** File > New > General Templates (found in the sidebar on the right). Click on the template of your choice!

◊ **In Word 2007:** Microsoft Office Button (top left corner) > New, then click on Installed Templates.

There ya go! Easier than ironing!

SPREAD SHEET BASICS

Excel In a Nutshell!

SPREAD SHEET BASICS

Spreadsheet basics

Computer spreadsheets are designed with accounting in mind, and if they were just limited to that, you could think of it simply as an accountant's ledger. But they do so much more!

On the next few pages well learn the basics in:

◊ **Microsoft Works Spreadsheet**

◊ **Microsoft Excel 2002**

◊ **Microsoft Excel 2007**

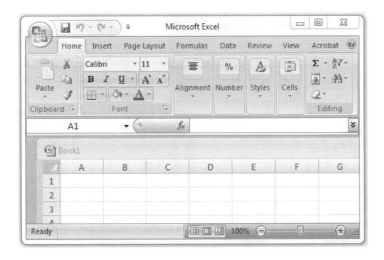

Here is an example of what Excel 2007 looks like.

Commands in Office 2007 programs are grouped together under headings. The headings are shown on Tabs in the top row; Home, Insert, Page Layout etc.

Spreadsheet basics

The Works Spreadsheet and Excel 2002,
look quite a bit alike.

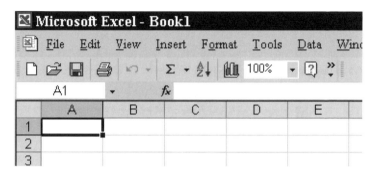

Spreadsheets are all about the grid.

Each cell (box) in the grid has a name assigned to it
because of its location.

For instance, the cell in the very top left is named A1.
The cell beside it, B1. Can you figure out where cell
C2 is? Or where cell E3 is?

Notice that cell A1 has a box around it. That means
that the cursor is active in that cell.

*S*ee where it says **A1** in the space just above the top
left-hand cell? *That space ALWAYS reflects whatever*
cell your cursor is active in.

Spreadsheet basics

Here I have typed "LABEL" in cell B2. Notice that "LABEL" is also shown in a window above. This is the function window.

$$"fx"$$

f : for function

x : for whatever number you use

When your cursor is active in a cell, whatever is in that cell will automatically show up in this space.

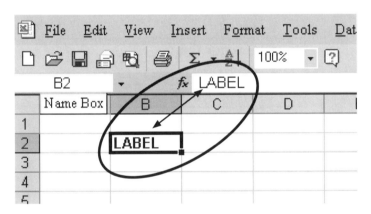

Whenever you learn a new program, you have to learn some new lingo that goes with it. Spreadsheets are no different. Here are a couple of new terms:

Label: the name of a cell with words in it.
Value: the name of a cell with numbers in it.

Knowing these two terms will make it easier to understand the instructions in Help, or when an *error* window pops up.

Common Formulas

When you use a spreadsheet for any math function, you have to create a formula to tell it what you want.

For example, you would enter the formula, =1+2 in a cell for the equation, 1+2=3. *Spreadsheets do the math for you. Any sort of math!*

Here is a list of math symbols found on your keyboard. You can use them to create formulas.

=	Equal
>	Greater than
<	Less than
>=	Greater than or equal to
<=	Less than or equal to
<>	Not equal to
+	Add
-	Subtract
/	Divide
*	Multiply
%	Percent
^	Exponent (to the power of)

**These symbols are also called
Arithmetic Operators, or, just Operators.**

You use a math operation (2+2) to solve a math problem, hence the operator in the middle of the numbers. You can have lots of operators in a problem. Remember problems like this? 6 + 3 - 4 x 8 =

Creating Formulas

Creating a Formula

If you want Excel to do math for you, you have to let it know your intentions. You have to let it know you are asking a question before you ask it.

How Confucius!

So, the equal sign = is placed in front of the question. While in regular math you write the *equation* 1+2= in Excel you would type a *formula* =1+2

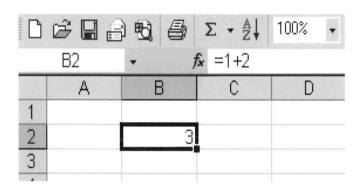

Here I typed =1+2 in Cell B2, then hit the Enter Key. **Notice that only the answer - or result - is in the cell. What I typed is showing in the** fx **(function) window.**

Results of formulas show **in the cells**
where they are typed.
You have to look back
in the formula window
to see what you actually typed in there!

Editing a Cell

EDITING A CELL

Once something is entered into a cell, the only way back into it is by typing directly into the formula window!

So, using the example on the last page, if I wanted to change =1+2 into =2+2, I would click the cursor into the formula window and make the change.

Practice! Try it out!
The best way to learn is to do.
So please, please, please!
Practice as we go along.

You don't learn to ride a bike
by reading about it!

Adding different cells together

Being able to use information in a variety of cells in whatever combination you need is one of the things that make a spreadsheet program so versatile.

Here I asked
cell C3 to figure the sum of cell A1 and B2

Editing a Cell

As soon as you hit Enter, the answer shows up in the cell. Notice that the formula (what I typed into the cell) is in the *fx* window.

C3		*fx* =(A1+B2)	
	A	B	C	D
1	7			
2		3		
3			10	

In this next example I changed the formula to subtract the cells, by changing the *operator*.
In the *fx* window, just change the **+** sign to a **-** sign!
You can change the operator anytime you like.
+ - / *

C3		*fx* =(A1-B2)
	A	B	C
1	7		
2		3	
3			4

Try it out! Practice! Follow along!

the AutoSum tool

Adding entire columns or rows — and a shortcut!

	A	B	C	D
1	72			
2	99			
3	23			
4	194			
5				

A4 ▾ f_x =SUM(A1:A3)

The AutoSum tool

AutoSum is a great tool, if you have a column, or a row of numbers that you want to total up.

Here's how to use it:
1. Click your cursor into the empty cell at the bottom of your column of numbers
2. Move your mouse and click on the AutoSum

Notice that the f_x window shows the formula. When you want to add many cells together you can use a colon (:). In this example, I've asked Excel to add cell A1 all the way through to A3, inclusively.

If you want to AutoSum a row, you have to highlight it first. Then with the cursor in the empty cell at the end, click on AutoSum.

Sorting lists

Sorting Data - Organizing a List.

Here's how:
1. Highlight the material you want to sort.

2. Move your mouse to Data > Sort

3. Choose how you want to sort. On the example, I made headings: Name & Age. You can sort by the columns too: A, B, C, etc.

Remember, you can always "undo" if you don't like what you've done!

Change your view!
with Excel 2002 & Works Spreadsheet,
click on View > toolbar
In 2002, keep "standard" checked and in Works, you can view larger icons!

That's spreadsheet basics in a nutshell. Play around with it and remember to save your work as you go along. That way if you mess up...

Bright Ideas

Internet Savvy

Seems the more I use my computer,
the more I expect it to do.
I feel the same about the internet.

Although using the internet is easy, not
letting it waste your time is another matter.
More importantly, you need to know how
to keep you and yours safe!

INTERNET SAVVY

Phishing

Internet Phishing
Not nearly as nice as fishing! This phishing is nasty.

It's about counterfeit web sites.

Internet Phishers try to trick you onto their counterfeit web sites, often with an email that looks very official.

The email will tell you to click on a link and enter some personal information. NEVER DO THIS!

Reputable companies will never send you an email asking for information they should already have — or ask you for your password! NEVER!

Your internet browser should offer phishing protection. Be sure that this tool is turned on.

**Keep your browser updated
to have the latest protection offered!**

A web browser is the program on your computer that lets you surf the internet.

Some of the most popular browsers are:
Internet Explorer, Mozilla Firefox, Google Chrome, Opera and, if you are using a Mac — Safari.

Internet Security

Once upon a time, not too very long ago, trusting that you were speaking privately on a telephone required a leap of faith!

You might even need a little leap of faith to trust the internet.

But, when you are ready to buy goods online with a credit card, or do online banking, you should do it with **more than faith.**

You should enter this world with a bit of know-how.

So, on the next few pages we'll learn some of the essentials of internet security!

Security Basics

There are four important aspects when considering internet security:

1. ***A Firewall*** — Denies access to your computer from outside, uninvited guests.

2. ***Anti Virus Protection*** — Your best protection against known computer viruses from entering or leaving your computer.

3. ***Automatic Updates*** — Continually updates Firewall and Anti Virus programs.

4. ***128 Bit Encryption*** — Encryption is a way of scrambling information going between two computers. With encryption, digital keys are needed to send and receive the information. With 128 bit encryption the digital key combinations are in the millions.

Level of security for you

If understanding internet security is a little fuzzy, this might help clear things up. Consider the three little pigs...

The first little piggy: straw house, flimsy windows and door — No Security!

Remember what happened to him?

The second little piggy: a solid wooden house with a couple of locks, but the big bad wolf wouldn't have too much trouble breaking in. Only security here, a Firewall.

The third little piggy knew about the big bad wolf! He built a strong brick house with reinforced windows, deadbolts on the doors and an alarm system. Safe and secure. He's got current Firewall and Anti-Virus programs and does automatic updates. *Smart Pig!*

***You* should live in the third little piggy's house!**
When you bank online or use your credit card, you need even more security! And, the security has to come from *where and who you are dealing with.*

Security when banking

Your bank knows about the big bad wolf
and they won't let him in!

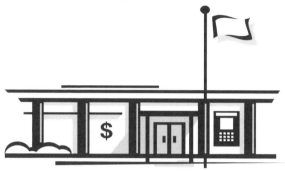

...locked steel doors, barred windows, guards...

Their computer, along with frequently updated Firewall and Anti Virus protection, uses secure 128 bit encryption for communicating.

Any time you give your credit card or other personal information, make sure the company you're giving it to uses encryption, 128 bit or higher!

There are two ways your computer will show you that you are using a secure site:

◊ The web address will start with **https://**
(an "s" at the end of http)

◊ A "locked" security icon will show in the task bar.

When you use the internet for banking or purchasing, ensure that you are communicating privately and securely.

Filtering internet content

Parental Controls

You may want to set *parental controls* on your computer to filter content such as offensive language, nudity, gambling, drugs etc. from being downloaded. **You can set some boundaries, using tools found in the** *Control Panel.*

In XP

◊ Control Panel> Internet Options> Content tab> Content Advisor > tick on, Enable

In Vista

◊ Control Panel > User Accounts and Family Safety

In Windows 7

◊ Control Panel > Parental Controls

You will create a password for yourself and then be able to choose the level of content you will allow. You also have an option here to completely block certain sites, or to only allow certain sites.

For more information on content rating I suggest you have a look at the Family Online Safety Institute's **web site: http://www.fosi.org**

Downloading

You can download almost anything from the internet into your computer.

Besides thinking you are downloading something clean of viruses, you should also think about...

Download Speeds

How fast your computer is and whether or not you have a high-speed internet connection is something you should think about before you try to download a large file.

Keep your friends happy. Don't send large files to them *unless* you know their system is fast enough to receive it!

Data can only be received as fast as a modem can receive it.

Do you have a high-speed modem or do you use dial-up to access the internet? Dial-up is a slow connection.

If you have high speed, and your friend uses dial-up, don't email them large files.

Sending large files to a very slow modem can really bung up the receiver's system.

Pictures and movies can be large files.

About Downloading

Downloading

All types of files and programs can be downloaded. A program will contain many different types of files within it. All *programs* are *applications. Application files* all end with *.exe*

You don't really have to know about file types, but it's one of those things that make understanding your computer's quirks a little easier.

Here are a few common file types.

.exe	=	executable application
.jpg	=	image file
.gif	=	image file
.bmp	=	image file
.doc	=	Word document file
.docx	=	newer Word document file
.dll	=	needed to help applications
.txt	=	text file
.mp3	=	audio file
.wmv	=	windows video file
.pdf	=	Adobe portable document
.ppt	=	Power Point file
.xls	=	Excel file
.mpeg	=	movie file
.wpd	=	Word Perfect document
.zip	=	zipped file (super condensed)

About Downloading

Downloading

You will find lots of reasons to download files or programs from the internet. You might even need to download a new program to view or open a file.

Did you receive a .docx file and can't open it? If you are using an older version of Word, you have to download Microsoft's File Converter. When you tried to open the file, you might have been told this! Make sure you do all your regular Windows updates first, then download and install the File Converter! Then you'll be able to open .docx files!

Automatic downloads

Many programs are pre-programmed to update themselves.

You should always keep your operating system up to date. Windows 7, Vista and XP are all types of operating systems. Be sure that Windows is set to do Automatic Updates, *and* to install the updates once they are downloaded!!!

Firewalls and internet security programs darn well better be set to update themselves!

Programs do this by logging onto their maker's server, and automatically downloading any updates needed.

Keeping up to date is a good thing!

Before you download...

Think ahead!

◊ Know *where in your computer* you are going to put your download. I created a folder in my computer called Downloads.

◊ Make sure you have an anti-virus program. After I download a program or file, **before I open it,** I make sure my anti-virus program has checked it over.

◊ Know what type of system you are running. Windows 7, Vista, Windows XP, etc. Will what you are downloading work with your system?

◊ Consider how big the program or file is. How long will it take to download through your modem?

◊ Is it a free download or do you have to pay for it? Will you need your credit card handy?

After you click on a *download now* button, a window will pop up that:

◊ Will show the name of the file. This often is not the name of the program. Write down the name of the file or change it to something more appropriate — don't forget about its file extension!

◊ It will suggest what folder it wants to download into. *Note that too! Nothing worse than looking for something you just downloaded!*

Temporary Internet Files

Temporary Internet Files or Cache

If you are browsing the internet, your computer will be downloading little bits and pieces all the time without you even knowing it.

These little bits are called *Temporary Internet Files* or *Cache*. They help web sites load faster the next time you visit them.

Many browsers will let you set how much internet cache to accept. And, like your trash, you should empty your cache once in a while.

In fact, you should absolutely clear your cache or temporary internet files after doing any online banking!

_____

_____ _____

_____

_____

_____

_____

_____

_____

Banking online

Every day, more and more people are enjoying the benefits and ease of banking online. Why? No long line-ups, instant access to your accounts, easy bill payments, the ability to transfer funds between accounts, even viewing investment portfolios!

The best part of banking online is that it's simple!

Banks want their customers to use this service, so they have made it user friendly. Some banks will charge for the service but many banks offer online services for free (it's included with your regular banking fees, whether you use it or not!).

I talked earlier about secure sites and 128 bit encryption. Any reputable bank uses 128 bit encryption for internet services.

Like most other things in life, banking involves trust. Trust your bank, but ask about encryption, account security and fraud protection before you sign on!

Banking online

Different banks will have different-looking web pages, but for the most part they offer the same services.

Here are a few of the most common services:

◊   Real-time access to account balances

◊   Bill paying

◊   Transferring funds between accounts

Here's what you need to sign up:

1. You must have a current account at the bank.

2. You will need your Social Security Number (USA) or Social Insurance Number (Canada).

3. You will need a valid email address.

4. Your browser must be able to handle 128 bit encryption.

5. You will be asked to create your own personal secret User ID and a secret Passcode.

Once you have these basic things, signing up is easy. Just follow your bank's online instructions!

Banking online

You're all signed up. Now what?

You will find that banking online is pretty straight forward.

Go to your bank's web site and "sign-on" in the space provided. You might need your user name and a password, or you might just sign in with your account number and a password.

Once you are signed in, you can:

◊   See your account balances.

◊   View all of your accounts at one time.

◊   Do a variety of banking chores.

When you bank online, you hold all the strings when it comes to paying a bill. You say who, how much and when. If you want, you can even set up automatic bill payments!

There is a catch! The billing company must have a contract with the bank, allowing their bills to be paid there.

Most utility and large companies are registered with banks, but there is a good chance Joe's Plumbing isn't set up for online bill payment!

Pay your bills online

Pay your bills online! Here's how:

1. Log onto your bank's website.
2. Look for the link that reflects "Pay Bills Online".

You will have to "add" your billing companies to your online banking. Look for a button (link) on this page that reflects that.

3. Search for your billing company and place them on your list.

Once you've added a company, you can pay them!

4. Pick the company you want to pay.
5. Select your account you want to pay them from.
6. Enter how much of the bill you are going to pay.
7. Confirm the information.
8. Click on Pay.
9. The bank should give you a confirmation or *reference number. W*rite this number down on your bill. You can even print this page for peace of mind.

That's it!
I said once before, online banking is so easy.
You <u>are</u> starting to believe me, right?

**Over the page,
for one more important note on
SECURITY!**

Temporary Internet Files

I'm repeating myself a bit here, but if you missed it the first time, I hope you'll read it this time!

Your computer remembers the web sites you visit by storing not only the web addresses, but also little bits of information that make loading the site faster next time you visit it.
Your computer might also store passwords and log-in information.

You can remove this information from your computer by deleting your history and clearing your cache or deleting temporary internet files.

Not cleaning up the cache in your computer, after doing internet banking, can be just like leaving money on the table for a hacker!

This is why it is important that,
after you log-off from your bank,
you clear your computer's
Temporary Internet Files (or Cache).

Here's how:
Start > Control Panel > Internet Options

Click Delete in the Browsing History area.
If you are asked if you are sure you want to delete these files — say yes!

Protect yourself

Good Practices...

Have you heard of the term "hacker"? A hacker is someone who sneaks into a computer for information. An information robber, an identity thief.

It is not hard to protect yourself.

Here are a few tips for safe secure computing.

1. Always log-off at the end of your online banking session.

2. It's a good practice to close your internet browser after doing online banking. This will ensure you are logged off. This is a good idea if you have just used your credit card online too. *Especially if you are on a public computer!*

3. Close your browser when you are not using the internet.

4. Safeguard your User ID, PIN and/or Password.

5. Banks will NEVER send you an email asking for personal or account information. BE AWARE of phishy emails. (Or phishy phone calls!)

6. NEVER send personal or account information via text messaging or email.

7. Keep your computer up to date! Do all the Windows updates. Keep your Anti-Virus and Anti-Spyware up to date. Make sure you are using a Firewall.

8. Don't click on Pop-up ads: so many are full of spyware.

Bright Ideas

EBAY! The world's largest virtual garage sale!

OK, so maybe it's an Auction House, but I've always thought of it as a garage sale — something I'm more familiar and comfortable with!

Like any garage sale, you can stroll in and browse at all the items. If you see something you like you can look at it a little closer. If you REALLY like it, you're going to have to introduce yourself to the seller, and make them an offer!

eBay is not complicated and is set up to give the buyer and the seller confidence. It is world-wide and browsing is free. Here are some of the basics we'll cover on the next few pages:

◊ Where is eBay?

◊ How to search for items by category

◊ To buy or sell, register with eBay

◊ How to buy

◊ How to sell

Where is eBay?

Where is eBay?

www.ebay.com is based in America, www.ebay.ca is based in Canada, www.ebay.de is based in Germany...

eBay is all over the world. Each country follows standard practices that have made eBay what it is, a service built on trust. They are connected, in that once you are registered with one, you are registered with all.

Ebay sellers are just like you.
There isn't a big eBay warehouse!

You can find almost anything on eBay.

In fact, it's easy to find *too much* of what you're looking for, so...

Here are some tips to make searching easier!

Searching eBay

It's easier to learn by doing, so…
Let's practice!
Please log on to www.ebay.com

1. **Let's search for a TV.** Today, as I write this, I searched for "television". eBay found 210,677 items. Then I tried "tv" and it came up with 164,418 items. Yikes!

2. Notice in the left side-bar, "Categories". This can help you narrow down your search. I chose to narrow my search down to "electronics", now it shows 57,504 items. Still, Yikes!

3. The left side-bar now offers ways to narrow down your search even more by showing you sub-categories to choose from. It's showing Televisions, 15, 202. Once I click on that I see many other choices to narrow my search by.

4. I chose: Portable, LCD monitor technology, HD Ready. **8 Items!** — *Now this is a number I can deal with!*

So, what did we learn? Be Precise!
Search for what you want.

eBay - What's that mean?

Items listed on eBay are updated every hour. The lists are ordered by date, the most current being first. *Regular eBay users qualify to purchase an option that will promote their item to the top of the list.* What you find one hour, you might not find the next.

Items are listed, described briefly, and categorized under these headings:

Compare	You can tick multiple items that you're interested in, and then eBay will create a new list showing only these items.
Item Title	What the seller has chosen to name their item.
Price	Shows the asking price, minimum acceptable price (reserve) and current bid. "Buy it now" means that if you pay that price, it's yours!
Bids	The number of bids that have been placed on an item.
Time Left	Shows the length of time the listing has left.

If you see something you're interested in, click on its picture or title to see more information.

Tip:
Use the BACK button on your browser to return to previous screens when surfing eBay.

eBay - What's that mean?

If you click on an item for more information, this is what you will see:

Starting Bid	The starting price the seller placed on the item.
Current Bid	Highest and most current bid on an item.
Time Left	Remaining time for the listing.
Start Time	The day and time the item was listed.
History	Lists the bidding history, which includes who and how much was bid. This is a good place to find honest comments from buyers and sellers.
Item Location	Where the item is physically located.
Featured Plus Listing	Featured Plus is the selling option that will bring an item *near* the top of the list.
Ships To	Where the seller is willing to ship to.
Shipping Costs	How much, by what method the item would be shipped.

Scroll down the page to find a *description* of the item. This is what the seller has written up to promote it.

The description area is a good place to discover if you are buying from a business or from a regular Joe down the street. Many businesses sell on eBay.

eBay, Sign-up

See something you absolutely must have?

To buy or sell anything,
you must register with eBay.

Don't worry, it's quick and easy to register.

HERE'S HOW

Click on the "Register Now" button to be led through a **3-step process**, asking you to:

1. Enter your personal information.

2. Create your User ID and a Password.

3. Confirm your registration.

eBay, Registering

Step 1, Personal Information

◊ You will be asked for personal information such as your name, phone number, address and email.

◊ Credit card information is not always required, but, in the event that you are asked...

Quoted from eBay.com

You will be asked to place your credit card on file if the email address you entered cannot be used to verify your identity. This usually happens for one of the following reasons:

1. *The email address came from a free, web-based account such as a Yahoo or Hotmail account.*

2. *The email address is invalid - that is, attempts to send a message to this email address repeatedly "bounce" back to eBay.*

End quote.

◊ You will be shown the User Agreement and Privacy Policy and have the choice to accept it or not.

◊ **If you do not accept** the agreement – you're done here, and no eBay buying or selling for you!

If you accept the agreement, you go on to Step 2!

eBay, Registering

Step 2, User ID and Password

◊ Create a User ID; it does not have to be your real name. Have a look on eBay and see what kind of user IDs people have. Choose an ID that you will remember.

◊ Choose a password.

◊ You will also be asked to create a *question and answer* that can be used to identify you if ever you forget your ID and password.

◊ If you forget your ID or Password, eBay will ask your secret question, among other personal stats, and then email the information to you.

> Tip
> If you have a notebook of ID's and passwords, keep it in a safe spot, away from your computer.
>   ..In case of a break-in.

Step 3, Confirming your Registration

Next, you will receive an email from eBay that asks you to confirm your registration.

◊ Make note of the *confirmation code number.*

◊ Click on the *Complete eBay Registration* button.

That's it.
You're ready to
shop on eBay!

eBay, Bidding & Buying

How do you pay?

The Seller determines how they want to be paid. Visa, BidPay, MasterCard, American Express, PayPal, personal check, money order and more; even cash! **I don't advise sending cash through the mail.**

Before you bid on an item, know these things:

◊ Be sure that you really want to buy an item before you place a bid.

◊ Look for a reserve price. Sellers often set a minimum price (the reserve) that must be met.

◊ Look for the shipping fees. Some items are priced very low and make up for it with high shipping fees! *Tricky people...*

◊ See what form of payment the seller will accept; make sure you're comfortable with that method.

◊ Where is the item coming from, and will the seller ship to your area?

◊ Notice if insurance is offered.

◊ Notice if they are new to eBay or have a history. If the seller has a history, check it out!

eBay, Bidding

You have found the item that you just must have!
Yippee!

Before you go ahead and bid on it, decide what your TOP dollar is going to be. You might be surprised just how much like an actual auction eBay can feel. It is very easy to get carried away! It's fun bidding on items, and even when the amounts climb at only 25 cents a bid, the quarters can add up pretty fast!

Here's how to bid:
1. Click on the item's title to open up the information page. Click on Place Bid.

2. Enter the dollar amount you want to bid in the *bidding window* that pops up.
   ◊ Notice the statement "You are agreeing to a contract…" by confirming the bid.

3. Click on *Confirm Bid* to see if your bid will be accepted. It might be good, or it might be beat out by a previous bid. Decide if you want to bid again.

4. If you have a winning bid, you will receive an email confirming your bid. If you get outbid, you'll get another email letting you know!

5. You can also ask the seller any question you have before you bid —how old is it, does it still have a warranty, how much for shipping to...?

You can also do **proxy bidding** – tell eBay your maximum bid, and they will bid for you.

You're the highest bidder!
You won! It's yours!
Now What?
$ $ $

1. eBay will send you an email: "Congratulations – You Are The Winning Buyer!"

2. Check for payment options and details within the email; follow the directions.

3. If the shipping amount is yet to be determined, the Seller might email and ask for a destination and then let you know.

4. The Seller will send the item once your payment is processed. If you pay with a check, they will probably wait till it clears.

> Remember, use the Back button on your browser to return to previous pages.

eBay, About selling

People shop on eBay for all sorts of reasons. They might be looking for a rare special item, or just be looking for a good deal. If you're selling something, think about who might want to buy it.

You'll find lots of selling tips on eBay. Some tips are just good suggestions. Other tips can be an added expense, such as eBay's *Featured Plus* program that puts your item near the top of the heap.

When you list an item for sale, eBay will charge you for the listing. Think of it like running a classifed ad in the newspaper. Instead of being charged per word, like you are with a newspaper ad, you are charged according to your selling price.

eBay calls this basic charge their Insertion Fee.

The Insertion Fee for an item starting at less than .99 cents US might only be 20 cents. If an item is selling for more than $500 US, the fee could be $4.80.

The fees vary a little with the times, and the fees vary from country to country.

eBay, Selling options

You will be asked — and tempted — to add options to help sell your stuff. Be careful you don't add options worth more than what you are selling!

If your item sells, you are also charged a **Final Value Fee.**

This is a percentage of the final bid.
Currently, items under $25 are charged 8.75%; over and above that $25, you'll be charged an extra 3.5%.
The percentage drops as the Final Value goes up.

Perhaps, the best advice I can offer, is to become familiar with eBay before you sell.

When you want to sell something, do a search for similar items. See how they are listed. Notice the category (s) the item is listed in and what similar things sell for.

eBay - Ready to sell

Here's how:

1. Log on to eBay with your User ID and Password.

2. If this is your first time selling, eBay will ask you to register as a seller.

3. You will be required to provide credit card information.

Now that you are a Registered Seller, these are the steps eBay will bring you through to list your item:

1. Choose a category(s) for your item. This is an important decision as people search for items by categories.

2. Choose a title for your item.

3. Give details about your item; add a picture if you like.

4. State your payment and shipping terms.

5. Review. Make any changes. Submit!

Easy like pie!

eBay Scammers

There are so many users on eBay, not only because they might want to make a quick buck, but because it's easy and fun.

But sadly, not everyone in our world is honest.

So, when you are surfing around, <u>use common sense</u>. If something looks quirky, it just might be. If it sounds too good to be true, there's a good chance it isn't.

Please, take time and look over the next couple of pages for a few simple tips, directly from eBay.

Knowing just a little can save you a lot!

DON'T BE SCAMMED BY
EBAY IMPERSONATORS.

The real thing is where it's at!

Security on eBay

Security on and about eBay

Please read the following information
quoted directly from eBay.com.
It is important information to know.

Email and Web Sites Impersonating eBay

◊ *eBay will never ask you to provide sign-in passwords, credit card numbers, or other sensitive information through email. If we request information from you, we will always direct you back to the eBay site. With very few exceptions, you can submit the requested information through your "My eBay" page.*

◊ ***Take caution with email that includes attachments or links***

◊ ***eBay will not send you email that includes attachments*** *and you will not be required to enter information on a page that cannot be accessed from the eBay site. If you receive a message that appears to have been sent from eBay that includes an attachment, do not open it.*

Security on eBay

Security on and about ebay

Continuing quote from ebay.com

Beware of fake Web sites pretending to be eBay

◊ *Only enter your eBay password on pages where the Web address (URL) begins with **https://signin.ebay.ca/**. Even if the Web address contains the word "eBay", it may not be an eBay Web page.*

◊ *These fake Web sites (also called "spoof" Web sites) try to imitate eBay in order to obtain your eBay password and access to your account.*

◊ *All genuine eBay.ca sign-in pages will begin with **https://signin.ebay.ca/**. Similarly, eBay.com sign-in pages will begin with **https://signin.ebay.com/**.*

◊ *Never type your eBay User ID and password on a page that doesn't have "ebay.ca" or "ebay.com" immediately before the first forward slash (/).*

End quote from eBay.com

Instant Messaging

Instant Messaging, Abbreviated *IM*

Text messaging, instant messaging and chat rooms: seems like everyone is doing it! So, what are they?

◊ **Text Messaging** - small text messages sent between cell phones. Receiving text messages is often free, but sending them costs a small amount. The fee is maybe around 15 cents. This wee amount can add up incredibly fast, so if you are watching pennies, be careful! Many companies offer unlimited text plans.

◊ **Instant Messaging** - when you're using an IM program, you can type back and forth to friends in real time! You can IM in Facebook & Messenger.

◊ **Chat Rooms** - Chat rooms are for groups of people with similar interests. You can instant message between the group, or post a message that people can respond to on a message board.

Instant Messaging Safety

Is IM safe?

For your computer?
Mostly yes. I say "mostly" only because IM is so popular. Inevitably there'll be viruses written with IM in mind...

A best defence is a good offence.

Your computer needs to have current anti-virus software and anti-spyware software running. Your IM program should also be up-to-date and you should keep your Microsoft Windows updated too!

Most viruses are transmitted through attachments and *you have to open the attachment for it to be released.*

The best way to be safe from viruses is to delete messages with attachments!

Of course, friends will send you attachments. If you wonder about the attachment, email your friend and ask them if they sent you something — before you open it! Once opened, it's too late to stop a virus.

Instant Messaging, Stay Safe

Is IM safe for very young children?

NO, not without proper supervision and guidelines.

You would never drop a child off in the middle of Times Square without any supervision. Well, letting them go into IM without guidance is just about as bad!

You have to learn about internet safety, and you must teach your children how to use the internet safely.

Safety Tips and IM Etiquette

◊   Don't open attachments

◊   "Block" uninvited messages

◊   Only IM with people you personally know

◊   A Webcam - best used on a computer in the living room or kitchen - not a good idea in the privacy of a bedroom....

◊   IM addresses are NOT anonymous. They are traceable. It is illegal to make threats or elicit something bad. The police can *and will* track down illegal behavior.

◊   Understand that messages can be copied and forwarded on to other people. Emailing is NOT PRIVATE. Emails can last forever. Be careful what you say. *Be Kind. You Can't Rewind.*

Instant Messaging, Stay Safe

Safety & Etiquette

◊ People often change their "handle" (nickname) or will have more than one account in different names. **Be sure you know who you are really talking to.**

◊ Feelings are easily hurt through IM, especially when kids are chatting back and forth. Something as simple as "Did you see what Mary was wearing today?", can turn into something pretty ugly.

◊ Think about what you are saying — and what you are not saying. Remember, the reader can't see your face or hear the inflection of your voice. Abbreviated text can easily be misunderstood!

◊ IM etiquette can be summed up by my Mom's simple rule. *Treat others with the respect and dignity that you expect to be treated yourself.*

Now that I've said all that...
Using IM is really kinda fun :-)
and a very efficient way to communicate!

Instant Messaging, Sign-up!

How to start
Most PC's come with an Instant Messaging program pre-installed. <u>You just have to open it, and then register with the service</u>.
Basic IM services are free. If you want something with more options, you'll have to pay for it.

Here are some of the most popular instant messaging programs:

 Windows Messenger
(MSN, Hotmail, Windows Live)

 Facebook has IM — check out
Chat on your Facebook page

 AIM, from America Online

Signing up
The process is very easy. Deciding on a screen name or email name can be the hardest part. Well, maybe not. Finding a name that is not already being used, that can be the hardest part!

The registration information is basic. You will be asked for your name, gender, birthdate, an alternate email address, and you will need to come up with a password to access your account.

Once a screen name has been accepted, you're in!

Instant Messaging

Signed up!... Now what?...   Find friends of course!
Let your friends know that you have IM and give them
your IM email address. Add your friends' addresses to
your "contact" list.

You will find sending and receiving messages is very
straightforward. If it wasn't, nobody would use it!
Type a message and hit send!
"Beep" — you got one back! Simple as that.

When you have your IM program open, you will
receive messages from friends as soon as they send
them. It is very much like using a telephone, but
with text. Unlike your phone, you can have many
conversations going on at once.

You can even have your program open and not accept
messages, by changing your "status". Instead of
being online, you can be: away, appear offline, out to
lunch... there's lots of options.

Every program has a different layout, but they all
essentially DO the same things. Have a look through
the options. Turn on or off sounds, set up what security
levels you want, change your nickname. Look around.
Check out your options. Don't be scared!
Have fun!

Chat Rooms

When you text-message or IM with someone, you are communicating one-on-one. When you use a "chat room" everybody in the *room* sees what you have to say.

IM programs have an option to create a personal chat room with your friends, great for making plans! If, during a conversation, you want to "invite" someone to join in, you can. Just have a look around for the invite option.

Chat rooms are a great place for public discussion. People getting together virtually, offering help and sharing lots of new ideas. It's really very cool.

If you "meet" someone in a **public chat room** and decide to get to know them better, be careful. You don't really know the person. You only know what they have typed or told you, and it might not be true.

Never personally meet a stranger alone. Bring a friend, tell other friends what you are doing. Meet in public. Be street-smart and stay safe.

About Facebook and Such!

Have you heard about Facebook or MySpace? Are you wondering what they are all about?

They are social networking websites.
"Social" being the keyword! Facebook and MySpace are currently two of the most popular sites, but there are hundreds of other networking sites out there.

They are a great way to stay connected with your friends or to communicate between co-workers or community groups.

When you join, your own personal web page is created for you. It features information about you, that you give when you register! This home page, or personal "Profile" can usually be modified to show as much, or as little, information about yourself as you like.

Think of your Profile page as a personal stage.
A stage with audience participation!

About Facebook

I'm going to use Facebook as an example of what to expect when you join a networking site.
If a friend invites you to join another network, you will find that they work along the same lines...*mostly!*

Once you join, you will be able to search for your friends and ask them to be part of your network — or networks. You might be surprised to see how fast you can connect with old friends!

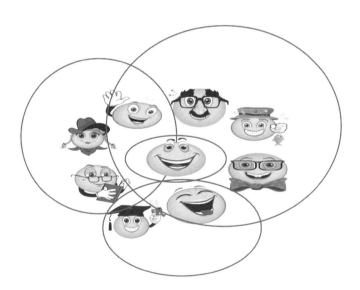

After the registration form is completed, Facebook will send a confirmation email to an address you provided.

Clicking on the confirmation link, in this email, completes the registration process.

Facebook Signing up

Go to www.Facebook.com

All you need to sign-up on Facebook is a valid email address.

Sign Up

It's free and anyone can join

First Name:

Last Name:

Your Email:

New Password:

I am: Select Sex: ▾

Birthday: Month: ▾ Day: ▾ Year: ▾

Why do I need to provide this?

Sign Up

Create a Page for a celebrity, band or business.

Facebook asks all users to provide their real date of birth to encourage authenticity and provide only age-appropriate access to content. You will be able to hide this information from your profile if you wish, and its use is governed by the Facebook Privacy Policy.

Next, when you personalize your settings, it is a good idea NOT to show your whole birthday on your public Facebook page. Birthdates are often used as a security question to verify who you are.

Facebook, Signing up

After you fill out that intial page, the next page will verify that you are a person and not a computer by asking you to type in a couple of squiggly words that are shown. **The Next 3 Steps get you going!**

Step 1, Find Friends!
This is easy if you let Facebook have access to your email address book. It only takes a second and you can pick and choose who you want to invite to be your friend.

◊ First it will find your friends who are already on Facebook. It will send them a notice that you've joined and ask them to be your friend. They will have a choice to confirm you as a friend or to ignore your request.

◊ Then it will show a list of your contacts that are not on Facebook. You can then choose to send them an invitation to join if you like.

Step 2, Profile Information
You can tell as much or as little about yourself as you want in your profile.

◊ There are spaces open that you can fill in or leave empty. What you share is entirely up to you.

◊ The *people you may know* page shows some friends of your friends that you may want to become friends with!

Step 3, upload a Profile Picture! Or skip if you want.

That's it, you've joined!

Facebook, Welcome

Welcome to Facebook!
The first time you sign on you'll be on Facebook's Welcome page where you can edit your profile more. Every time after that you will open to your regular Facebook page.

You can always edit anything on your profile page, including who sees what! Click on Account, found on the right side of Facebook's header.

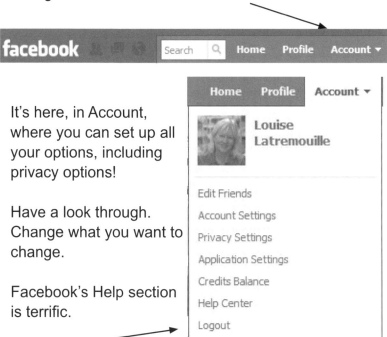

It's here, in Account, where you can set up all your options, including privacy options!

Have a look through. Change what you want to change.

Facebook's Help section is terrific.

LOGOUT
of Facebook when you are leaving your page.
ESPECIALLY if you are on a public computer!
The next time you sign on, you will have to use your password and the email address you signed up with to get back in.

Facebook, Profile & Privacy

Think about what you show and tell on Facebook.
And, if you have kids on Facebook,
be aware of what *they show and tell* on *their* profile!

Teach safe practices!
"Think Before You Post"

Consider these questions, compiled by the organisers of Safety Internet Day, before your next posting, and if you're a parent, ask your children these questions to help them learn about responsible posting:

◊   Are you using the privacy settings offered by social networking services? On Facebook, you can always adjust them on the Privacy Settings page.

◊   Are you selecting friends online that you can trust? Remember it's not just about what you post, but how others may use that content.

◊   Are you carefully thinking about the potential consequences of publishing your photos before you upload them?

◊   Do you ask for permission from your friends before publishing photos of them? A photo that may be funny to you may cause harm for a friend.

"Think Before You Post" is a positive message. It is about taking control of your online safety and participating in the benefits of social media, with respect for yourself and for others.
Quoted with permission, from Facebook's Safety Blog.

Facebook, Your Page

There are 3 icons along the top of Facebook's header.

◊   The left one is to help you find friends.

◊   The middle one is for Facebook email messages.

◊   The one on the right is for Facebook notifications.

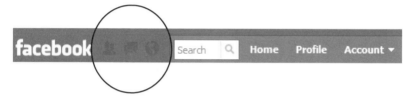

You can email between Facebook friends. You cannot email from Facebook to an address or person that is not on Facebook.

You can control what kind of notifications you receive in your account settings.

When someone requests you to be their friend, you'll see an alert by the friend icon.

The look and layout of Facebook may change with the times; after all, updating and change is good. So, if Facebook has done a facelift since I wrote this book, you might have to look around on the header or sidebar to find exactly what you want.

Facebook, Your Wall

Your Wall is your Profile Page.
Through your Account settings, you can control who can view or write on your wall. It can be open to: Only Friends, or Friends of Friends, or Everyone.

In this example there are two tabs, Wall and Info. If you upload pictures, then you will see a Photo tab; upload a video and you'll see a Video tab.

You must be on your own Profile page to upload pictures or videos to your wall.

You can type in the little window, where it`s asking, `What's on your mind?" This area is called your Publisher.

Click on the icons right below the publisher space to add photos, videos, links to other websites, or a link to a special event.

You can use these same icons to post pictures or videos on your friends' walls! And yes, if you don't say otherwise in your account settings, they can post pictures and videos on your wall too!

Facebook, Getting Around

Getting around on Facebook is easy.

News Feed is your Home page. It is where you will see what your friends are are up to.
When you logon, Facebook will open up on the News Feed page.

Click on *Profile* along the header bar to go to your Profile page and your wall.

Click on the headings in the left sidebar to have a peek at all you've got going on.

If any of your friends are Online, you will see their name listed here. Just click on their name to chat with them. If someone is trying to chat with you, you might hear a little ping.
Find Chat at the bottom right corner of Facebook.

Bright Ideas

Twitter

Everyone's all a Twitter...

What is it and why is it so hot?

Twitter is
instant messaging (IM) to the masses.
IMs of no more than 140 characters!

> Just how much can you say in
> only 140 characters?..What I've
> typed here in this box is just
> that! Characters include spaces
> and puncutation.

A Twitter IM is called a Tweet!

It's hot, because it's quick and easy — and immediate.
For instance, Twitterers had tweeted about the big
earthquake in Haiti before the News stations knew
what was happening!

Can twitterers be a word?

Twitter

Twitter is also very mobile. You can send and receive messages on both your computer and mobile devices.

Twitter in itself is free to use. But, if you are using it on your cell phone, your texting charges will show up on your cell bill.

If you are going to twitter on your cell, its a good idea to have an "unlimited" text account.

You don't even have to join
to view what's happening on Twitter.
Go to
www.twitter.com

On the bottom of Twitter's home page you'll see a whole bunch of topic headings. Twitter calls these Trends. **Trends are the hot topics**, what people are twittering about the most.

All *tweets* go through Twitter's server and Twitter looks at every incoming tweet. Then they rank them in popularity.

You can check out what's popular by the minute, by the day and by the week.

*Twitter is very current!
And, Very Public!*

Sign up to Tweet

Go to www.twitter.com and fill out this form.
It's really this easy to sign up.

Hardest part might be coming up with a Username!
Usernames are what people will know you as on
Twitter. It could be your own name (without spaces) if
it is not already taken, or you can make something up.
I'm "MyParentsTweet" on Twitter.

*BTW (By the way) having to type in those squiggly
words is a way of confirming that you are actually a
person, not a computer, signing up.*

Once you have joined, you can click on Profile and tell
a little about yourself (in 140 characters or less!).

Who to Tweet with

Home Profile Find People Settings Help Sign out

You will see this header when you are on your
Home page or looking at your Profile.
Click on Settings to change your Profile
Be sure to SAVE YOUR CHANGES when u r done.

Twitter is a community of conversations.
You can **follow** the conversations, or you can join in.

Find People
When you click on Find People you'll see 4 headings:

Find accounts and follow them.

Browse Suggestions	Find Friends	Invite By Email	Find On Twitter

Twitter KIS (Keeps it simple). The short, simple layout
under each of these tabs makes it easy for you to
make connections.

The folks at Twitter even give us great tips on what's
what! This tip was on the Browse Suggestions page
the day I wrote this!

 Browse Suggestions

Select the topics you are interested in. Find a few people you want to hear
from, then follow them. When you **"follow"** someone, each time they tweet,
you'll see their tweets on your Twitter Home page. You can follow or unfollow
sources anytime.

Finding Twitter friends

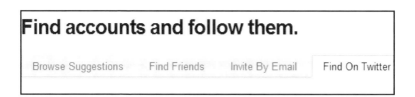

Find accounts and follow them.

Browse Suggestions   Find Friends   Invite By Email   Find On Twitter

When you Follow someone, each time *they* tweet you will see it on *your* Twitter home page.

You can follow topics or people that interest you, or you can choose just to follow your friends and family.

Tweeting can create a feeling of connection. For example: Our son lives across the country from us and sometimes I find it hard, him being so far away. But receiving his tweets about little everyday things, like "out for groceries" or "studying for a mid-term", makes me feel like he's not so far away. It's being part of the ordinary that can make you feel connected.

Sometimes the Twitter server gets too busy and you get to see the "Fail Whale"!

Don't worry, Twitter doesn't take long to recover.

Twitter Account Settings

Home Profile Find People Settings Help Sign out

Click on Settings and set all your preferences.
It's here that you can *Protect Your Tweets* if you want.
This feature can help to keep your tweets private.

Here are more great Twitter tips that you'll find on the
Settings page.

If you are using
Twitter on a public
computer, be sure to
Sign Out when you
are done!!!

Twitter Etiquette:
Tweet respectfully.
Follow with interest.
UnFollow kindly.
Don't Spam.
Report Spam.

Then there's Mom's
rule: If you don't have
anything nice to
say, then don't say
anything at all.

Account

From here you can change your basic
account info, fill in your profile data,
and set whether you want to be
private or public.

Tips

Filling in your profile information will
help people find you on Twitter. For
example, you'll be more likely to turn up
in a Twitter search if you've added
your location or your real name.

Change your Twitter user name
anytime without affecting your existing
tweets, @replies, direct messages, or
other data. After changing it, make
sure to let your followers know so
you'll continue receiving all of your
messages with your new user name.

Protect your account to keep your
tweets private. Approve who can
follow you and keep your tweets out
of search results.

Twitter @reply or ReTweet

Twitter is evolving. The folks at Twitter add, change and delete features as it grows.

Just a bit ago Retweeting (or RT) was done by the masses, but wasn't an official Twitter feature. Now it is! We'll just have to wait and see what comes next!

When you hold your mouse over someone's tweet, you will see two options appear: Reply and Re-Tweet.

What is a Retweet?
A Retweet is a reposting of someone else's tweet onto your home page. The original Tweeter is given credit for the post.

What is a Reply?
If I replied to someone's post, it would look like @MyParentsTweet — then what ever I said. The reply would show up on both their home page and my own.

Direct Messaging?
A Direct Message is a Twitter email. You can send a direct message to someone you follow and who follows you.

When you receive a DM (direct message) you will see a notice of it in the sidebar, on the right side of your home page.

What's bit.ly/bGfx01?

No, I'm not swearing there...

You will see all sorts of these funny looking links all over Tweets. They are shortened URL's (web site addresses). There are a number of companies that do this but Twitter recently partnered up with a company called Bit.ly. Find them at, http://bit.ly

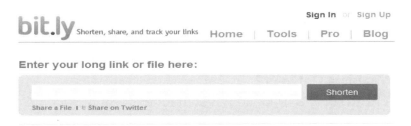

It's phenomenally easy to use! Just enter the long web site in the space provided, click on Shorten, and whammo — you've got a bit.ly shortened link!

Why would you need this? Well some links are crazy long and if you're only allowed to use 140 characters... Here's Bit.ly's explantion of what they do.

What is bit.ly?

bit.ly is a utility that allows users to shorten a long URL, share it, and then track the resulting usage.

For example, you can turn this link:

http://maps.google.com/maps?
f=d&saddr=New+York+Penn+Station&daddr=9th+Ave+%
26+14th+St,+New+York,+NY&hl=en&geocode=&mra=ls&dirflg=r&date=11%2F12%
2F08&time=4:13pm&ttype=dep&noexp=0&noal=0&sort=&sll=40.746175,-
73.998395&sspn=0.014468,0.036392&ie=UTF8&z=14

Into this link:

http://bit.ly/CUjV

This makes it easier to include the link in an email or Twitter post without it breaking or taking up too much space.

What's happening?

"What's happening?" That's the gist of Twitter.

I love this quote from Twitter's creator, Jack Dorsey, about how they came up with the name. Initially they thought of Twitch, but that didn't create nice imagery...

> "...So we looked in the dictionary for words around it, and we came across the word 'twitter,' and it was just perfect. The definition was 'a short burst of inconsequential information,' and 'chirps from birds.' And that's exactly what the product was."
> —Jack Dorsey

Twitter has only been around since 2006 and it is evolving as fast as it is growing in popularity.

Although about half of the tweets are just yakking between followers, the other half is full of news and useful information. So whether you just want to tweet between friends or tweet out to the world, Twitter is a nice place to be.

Skype!

Skype's amazing! It lets you talk to anyone in the world who is also on Skype — for free. Computer to computer.

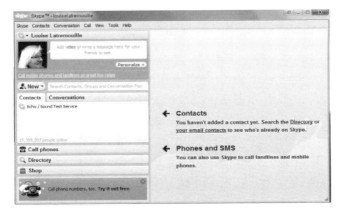

You can even use Skype to call a cell or landline phone, for a small monthly fee or by buying some Skype credit. Skype credit stays active for 180 days from the last time you used it. After 180 days of inactivity any remaining credit is gone.

Skype's monthly fees are incredibly reasonable.*
Only $2.95 for unlimited calling in the US and Canada.
$5.95 for unlimited US, Canada plus one more country.
A $12.95 month-to-month plan, gives you what Skype calls their World package. They have 40 countries in this package that you can make unlimited calls to!
These were the fees when I wrote this!

Skype's free services include:
Skype to Skype calling
Instant Messaging and Texting
Free Video Calls
Free Voice Mail

Skype, download & signup

- **Free** video calls

- **Free** Skype-to-Skype calls

- **Great rates** to landlines and mobiles

- **Easy** texting

- **Free** instant messaging

- **Voicemail**

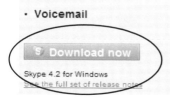

Skype 4.2 for Windows
See the full set of release notes

Putting Skype on your computer is extremely easy.

◊ Go to www.Skype.com
◊ Click on the Download tab
◊ Click on Download now

When the download is complete, choose Run to start the installation.

Skype will open up in a minute or two when the installation is complete. Then, first things first, you will create a Skype account by filling out this small form.

Next, you can fill out a couple of things on a profile page, like what country you're in and maybe your city. This information will help other people find you.

That's it!
Now, to find your friends on Skype!

Skype, find friends

Click on the Directory, then type in the person's name you are looking for. I find the best way to find someone though is by using their email address instead of their name.

You don't have to use your real name when you sign up, but you do have to use a real email address!

This next page helps you confirm you found the right person.

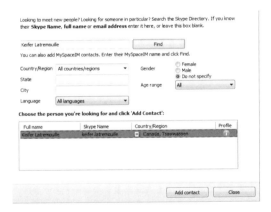

The new contact will receive a request to add you as a contact. They can accept or refuse you as a contact. Until then, they'll appear offline in your contact list.

Skype, make a call

Once you have established a contact, you can Skype with them. Click your mouse over their name in your contact list. You'll notice 3 tabs on the right pane.

Skype — for making a computer call.
Mobile — to make a call to their cell phone.
Home — to make a phone call to their landline phone.

To make a Skype to Skype call, just click on the *Call or Video Call* buttons and Skype places the call. If they don't answer, you can leave a message if you like.

Skype also has great Instant Messaging and Chat features. *Sometimes, if VOIP (Voice Over Internet Protocol) isn't working as well as it should during a Skype voice call, I'll supplement our talking conversation by using chat!*

Skype is really THIS easy!
Don't be afraid to try out Skype!
It's Fun & Its Free!

Bright Ideas

Beyond the Computer...

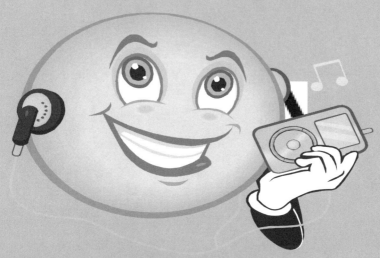

Mp3 players,
digital cameras
Cell phones...

Technology changes so fast. It's very exciting, but can also be a little frustrating.

The next few pages will simplify some of today's most common digital devices!

Beyond the Computer...

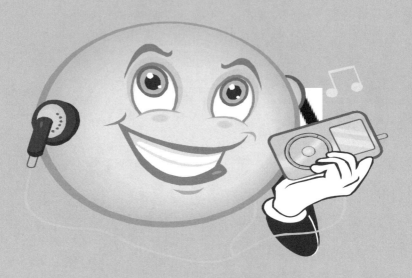

Cell phones

Having a cell phone is not only a convenience, it can also offer a measure of safety by giving you a way to call for help in case of an emergency.

But I swear, learning a new cell phone is one of life's most frustrating things....

On the next few pages I'll offer some tips on getting a cell phone, and try to make using them a little easier.

There are tons of companies out there looking to sell you their cell phone packages. Before you even go to the store, think about these things.

◊ The cell carrier you choose should have good coverage in the area you will be using it the most.

◊ What will you use your cell for most? Will it be for texting, phoning, email, music...?

◊ If phoning, what time of day would you use it most? Daytime minutes cost more than nighttime minutes. How many hours might you use it per day? Cell usage is charged by time used.

◊ Do you want to buy a pre-paid phone, or would you like to sign a term contract for a better rate and maybe a free phone?

Cell Phone Features

Here are a few of the options to think about when selecting a phone:

◊ Is it comfortable in your hand and easy to open, answer a call and hang up from a call?

◊ Are the # keys big enough for you? Do you need the keypad to be textile (Braille-like)?

◊ Is the display large enough to see?

◊ Does the phone have all the bells and whistles that you'll need? Does it have too many? If you only need/want to phone and text, will the extra options on the phone make it harder to use?

◊ Does it have a SIM Card (Subscriber Identity Module)? SIM cards store your phone numbers, text messages and other data. If/when you get a new phone, you'll just insert the old SIM card into your new phone to keep all your personal data!

SIM cards can make traveling less expensive, by reducing long distance and roaming charges. For instance, if you live in Texas, but you're traveling in Alaska, your calls while you were in Alaska would be charged long distance or roaming fees — because your carrier is in Texas! You can buy a local pre-paid SIM card in Alaska, insert it in your phone and voilà — you're using a local network!

Cell Phone Features

◊ Do you want a Smart Phone? SmartPhones are cell phones with features like web surfing, mp3 players, email capability.... Some are practically like a mini computer!

◊ Is it T9 capable? T9 is a predictive text option that makes texting easier and faster.

◊ Does it have a camera? Does it shoot movies?

◊ Does it have a vibrate mode? Is it easy to adjust the volume of the ring?

◊ Is the battery easily charged? How long does it hold a charge? How expensive is the battery to replace? Some batteries are so expensive it is cheaper to buy a new phone!

◊ Is it hands free or Bluetooth capable? Does the hands-free adapter come with it, or is it an extra?

◊ Does it have a speakerphone and how easy is it to access that feature?

◊ Does it have GPS capability?

I think I could go on and on here!

Cell phones are being developed everyday with such a growing list of features it's dizzying. Thinking about these basic features might make it easier for you to decide on what you want or need.

Cell Phone Fees

Having a phone with all the fancy features might be really nice, but using those features doesn't come free! Cell plans range from the most basic to the sky is the limit. ***Think about what you want.***
Cell companies are awfully good at romancing us into paying for services we don't really need.

Here's a bit about cell phone fees:

◊ Should you "Pay-As-You-Go" or have a monthly plan?

◊ How many minutes of talking will you do? What's their number of daytime or nighttime minutes allowed?

◊ What are the texting fees? Do you want unlimited texts or are you allowed so many a month? Will you be charged for incoming texts?

◊ Web Access fees? Often you are charged per web site you visit — surfing can get expensive!

◊ Do you need Voice Mail, Caller ID, Call Waiting, 3-Way Calling? Each one of these services comes with a fee.

◊ What are the charges for things like downloading ring tones and various Apps (Applications like games or tools like Mapquest)?

◊ Long distance and roaming charges?

◊ Are there family plans?

Cell Phone Fees

◊ There are add-on fees to most plans. These might include System Access Fees, 911 fees, taxes... Find out what theirs are!

◊ What are the charges for using more time or texts than your plan allows? These can add up quickly.

◊ If you are offered free services for a few months and find you aren't using them, be aware of when that "free" period ends or be charged for them.

◊ If you need to get out of a contract, what are the cancellation fees? These are usually very hefty. *And, found in the fine print of the contract!*

◊ Activation Fees. Your first bill will inevitably come with Activation fees.

Bottom line...

Find a plan that suits what you need.

Don't let your money fly out the door!

Cell Tech Talk...

What did they mean when they said...

Roaming	Is the term used when you travel outside your carrier's home area.
SMS	Short Message Service, refers to texting.
MMS	Multimedia Messaging Service. MMS is designed to handle photos, video, audio and texting.
WLAN	Wireless Local Area Network, the protocol used for internet access.
WAP	Wireless Application Protocol, similar to WLAN
SIM	Subscriber Identity Module card. SIM cards identify you to your carrier so they can account for the time and services you use — to bill you!
Locked	Many carriers "lock" their phones by programming them to only work with the SIM card they provide. You can ask (or plead) with your cell provider if they will let you unlock your phone for travel.
Un-locked	An unlocked cellphone will recognize and work with any SIM card.
Bandwidth	How much data can be transferred through your network at once.
Bluetooth	Bluetooth is a technology that uses short length radio waves to create a wireless connection between two devices.

Cell Tech Talk

2G, 3G phone	2nd Generation, 3rd Generation... of the same model of phone.
CDMA & GSM	There are two main cellphone networks that ALL celllphone companies use, and they aren't compatible with one another!
	One is CDMA, Code Division Multiple Access. CDMA is popular in North America and parts of Asia.
	The other is GSM, Global System for Mobile communication. GSM is the most common cellphone standard outside North America, used by more than 2 billion subscribers in most countries around the world.
	A SIM card will be compatible with one network or the other — not both!

There, now you know more than most!

Texting

Companies have made texting easier!

Alpha

It used to be that the only option for texting was to multitap out the words on the number pad. You will see this method referred to as Alpha on most phones. When in Alpha mode and you want to type the letter A, tap #2 once; B, tap #2 twice; C, tap #2 three times.

To Alpha-tap out the word Parents, you would press:
7-2-777-33-66-8-777

T9 or Predictive Text

Try it, you'll like it!! T9, (Text on 9 keys) is installed on most new cellphones. Some companies give T9 a different name on thier phones, Predictive Text and Dictionary are common. T9 tries to predict what word you want.

Simply press out the word on the # keys, **but don't multi-tap**. T9 will figure it out by the end of the word. For instance, to text the word Parents, I would tap;
7-2-7-3-6-8-7

VERY IMPORTANT TIP!!
The first time you use T9, don't look at what's coming up on your display
until the word is done!
It can be confusing seeing the all other words
that appear before you're finished!

Texting

Changing between T9 and Alpha mode.

These are texting options and often you can't access the options until you are actually writing a text.

Once you've started a text, you will see "Options" somewhere on the phone's display. Press the button on your phone that points to "Options" and choose what you want. You will find it is not too hard to toggle between Alpha and T9 mode.

Here's a few other texting tips!

◊ When you finish a word, press the fwd key or space key (often the # key) to move on to your next word.

◊ To type a number when using T9, just keep holding the number key down until the number is displayed.

◊ In most phones the #1 has punctuation and emoticons. :-)

◊ Did you just receive a text from someone? Hit Reply to open a new text to that person.

Text Text Text...

If you Text a lot, you will want to have a cell phone package that includes unlimited texting.
If not, the few cents each text message costs, can really — REALLY — add up!

SPAM ALERT!
Beware! There is text message Spam! Want your horoscope texted to you every day? You better know if it might cost you 95 cents every time you receive one! It is good practice not to give out your number to strangers and NEVER GIVE OUT YOUR CELL NUMBER Online!

CUL8R@$*

Acronyms
As text messaging grows, and devices got smaller, a language of acronyms was born. Like it or not, it's probably here to stay.

Some acronyms are more common than others and some develop just between friends. Texting acronyms are shorthand for typers.

Have you figured out my shortand above yet?

Texting Acronyms

Here are a few acronyms and what they mean:

BF	boyfriend or best friend
B4	before
B4N	bye for now
BRB	be right back
CMON	come on
CU	see you
D8	date
DIKU	do I know you
F2F	face to face
FYEO	for your eyes only
GF	girlfriend
GI	google it
GTG	got to go
IC	I see
LOL	laugh out loud
NO1	no one
NW	no way
OMG	oh my gosh
PM	private message
POS	parent over shoulder
RL	real life
SUP	what's up?
TA	thanks a lot
TC	take care
UR	you are
zzzz	sleeping (or bored)

Personal Digital Assistants

PDA's - Blackberry, Treo etc.,

We used to call these things organizers or day-timers, but nowadays they just do so much more. Some have so many functions they are practically mini-laptops!

A couple of PDA's have the lion's share of the market. The **Blackberry**, made by RIM, the **Treo**, made by Palm and the **iPhone** by Apple.

They are very popular devices in the business community, especially for people who work on the road a lot.

Like most technology, figuring out how to use them the first time can be frustrating; but once you get the hang of it, you might really enjoy the options these little PDA's offer!

Bluetooth technology

Go Wireless!
You will often hear that a device has Bluetooth.
OK. Great. What is it?

Bluetooth is a wireless communications technology that allows devices to talk to each other using short-length radio waves.
Imagine your computer system set up without any cables. Wow! With Bluetooth technology it can be.

Wireless
is not
science fiction
any more!

One of the great things about Bluetooth is that many different manufacturers are using it. If a device has Bluetooth technology, it can be set up to work with almost any other device with Bluetooth.

For example; if you had a Xerox printer and a Sony camera, and both had Bluetooth technology, you could send your pictures directly to your printer without physically connecting any cables!

It might look funny when people are talking into thin air, but if they are wearing a Bluetooth earpiece, they are *probably* not talking to themselves! The earpiece is working together with a Bluetooth-enabled phone!

mp3 players

Remember when...

mp3 Players

Mp3 players are today's hottest way to have your favorite music, and it's no wonder why. These little devices, iPods and such, give you terrific sound and hold hundreds - thousands - of songs.

And, there aren't any moving parts, so they don't skip like a portable CD player does!

An iPod is the most popular brand of mp3 player and I'll refer to it now and again on the next few pages.

Boy oh boy, we've come a long way...

mp3 players

The Basics

Mp3 players work with a computer. They play music downloaded from a computer, and their batteries can be charged by a computer.

A computer is important. So, before we start with your mp3 player, let's have a quick look at your computer....

Your computer needs to have a couple of basic parts:

◊ A USB or Parallel port to plug the mp3 player into! Most computers have a few of these.

◊ Speakers! So you can listen to what you download from the internet!

◊ A Sound Card (If you have speakers that work, you have a sound card.)

◊ And, a program for music! *Like iTunes or Windows Media Player*

mp3 players

What's what?

Display screen

The Menu Wheel. Works like a mouse. Drag your finger around it and the highlighted line on the screen moves up, down, left or right.

Earbuds, or Headphones

The Select Button, in the centre of the Menu Wheel. Once you have what you want highlighted, click on this button to select it.

There is a "hold" button on an iPod. Use this to make sure you don't accidentally turn it on or off, or to hold the volume from changing. Like many things on an iPod, it's a versatile tool!

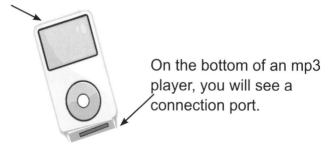

On the bottom of an mp3 player, you will see a connection port.

Different models might also have an on/off switch.

mp3 players

Connection Cable

One end of the cable connects to your mp3 player and the other to a USB port on your computer. Remember, from *My Parents First....* USB ports are ports that you can plug a variety of devices into.

With some models, you have to squeeze both sides of the connector to release it from the iPod. *(Took me a frustrated while to figure that one out...yanking on the cord... sheezzze!)*

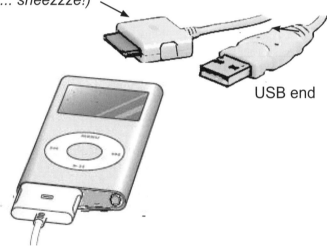

USB end

iPods and other mp3 players recharge when they are plugged into a computer. *The computer has to be turned on!*

Sync ... synchronize
"Sync" is a word used a lot.
It simply means the mp3 player and the music program on your computer are working together.

mp3 players

Putting music on your mp3 player.

Here's the skinny version:

◊ Mp3 players load music from a computer, so the first thing is to put music on your computer.

◊ Load music on your computer, either from a CD you own or via the internet.

◊ Having an internet connection is important.

◊ Connect your mp3 player to your computer.

◊ A music program will open that is sync'd with your mp3 player.

◊ Highlight the songs you want to put on your mp3 player.

◊ Choose "import" or "rip" (same thing) to copy the music onto your mp3 player.

◊ Eject and disconnect your mp3 player.

◊ Go for a nice walk and listen to your music.

mp3 players

Here's *how to do* the
how-to's on the skinny list!

**Here's how
to put music (mp3 files) on your computer.**

Mp3 players, play mp3 files. An mp3 file is a type of audio file that is very compact. So, putting lots of mp3 files on your computer won't take up much space on your hard drive.

First thing to do is to open your music program.

Wondering if you have a program for playing and downloading music in your computer?

The easiest way to find out what you have, is to put a CD into your CD drive, or plug in your mp3 player, and see what pops up!

An iPod uses a program called iTunes. Windows comes with Windows Media Player.

mp3 players

Saving music on your computer

Do you have your music program open?

Windows comes with Windows Media Player. Windows Media Player is great for working with all sorts of different brands of mp3 players.

When you purchase an mp3 player, it will most likely come with a disk. If you like, you can load its own program into your computer, but that's not always necessary.

An iPod uses iTunes. As soon as an iPod is plugged into a computer, it looks for iTunes.

When your iPod finds iTunes, it will try and "sync" with the program. This is great when you are on your own computer, because the music library you see on your computer screen is exactly what is on your iPod.

But, when you plug your iPod into another computer...Don't sync it to their iTunes! or, you will lose your music and gain theirs! Use the option to "manually manage" the music instead.

Remember, Sync means Synchronize!

mp3 players

Why having internet access is important

Music programs are made to work with the internet.

When you put a CD into your computer, the music program reads it and then goes to the www to find information about the CD, the artists and song titles.

You can import CD's to your computer without the internet, but each song (or "track") will be titled something like track 01, track 02, track 03, etc.

It's a lot of work adding song titles manually, but it's not hard to do. Just click your mouse over the track you want to name and the space will change into a box you can type in.

Your mp3 player loads music
from your music library!

A list or group of songs is called a playlist.

mp3 players

Connect your mp3 player to your computer.
What happens?
 The music program designed for your mp3 player will open — *as long as it's installed in your computer!*

When your program is open, have a look around. Get familiar with the screen. All music programs are laid out differently, but maybe this will help a bit:

<< > >>	Title of the song playing		
▼ Library	Name	Artist	Time
Your music can be sorted into categories, like: Artist, Year, Albums...	titles of the songs are listed here	the singer	length of a song
▼ Playlists			
Lists of playlists you have created. Just click on one to play it!			

There are more headings and more information, but I hope this will give you some idea of what you are looking at.

Find the
Rewind, Play & Fast fwd
symbols. Click on play,
>, and it will change to **II**,
which means stop or pause.

mp3 players

Every music program has these tools:
a **Ripper** and an **Encoder**

A Ripper

Ripping. The word sounds a little scary, but that's the term the music industry has used for years when copying music. So, you "rip" files from a CD *to copy the music* onto the hard drive in your computer.

Don't worry. You don't erase or affect the CD in any way, shape or form, when you *rip* music from it.

> **If you are using iTunes**,
> you won't see the term "Ripper"
> Ripping is simply called Importing.

An Encoder

Converts the music you are copying into mp3 files.

The music on CDs, is in a file format that is huge! The Encoder converts and compresses the songs into tiny .mp3 files. *Very clever thing, this encoder!*

If you are copying music for something other than an mp3 player, you can change the setting to encode into some other format.

If you want to change the encoding format with iTunes, you will find the Encoder within Preferences.

mp3 players

A little about audio (music) files.
Stuff you don't need to know, but knowing it can make things easier to understand!

Mp3 is an acronym for a type of audio file. It stands for Moving Picture Experts Group Audio Layer 3.
There, now you know more than most!!

Though mp3 files are the most popular, they are not the only kind of audio file around. Here are just a few others, and what the acronyms stand for.

.wma	Windows Media Audio
.wav	Waveform Audio
.aac	Advanced Audio Coding
.asf	Advanced Streaming Format
.vqf	Vector Quantization Format

...and then, there's MP4!
Mp4 was designed with sending videos in mind, but is evolving, as technology quickly does! Mp4 players are generally larger than mp3 players, with larger displays so you can *see* the videos!

What is great about mp4 technology is that it is designed to work with and support other formats!
It is also designed to grow, update and adapt to whatever is coming its way. *Pretty cool technology!*

146

mp3 players

Disconnecting your mp3 player

Before you disconnect your mp3 player, it is very important that you tell your computer that you are going to disconnect it. *(This is a good practice for many devices you connect to your computer — like a camera for instance!)*

You might see an eject or disconnect command as part of your music program, or you might see an icon for your device on your desktop. If you see an icon on your desktop, right-click over it and click *Eject* on the mouse menu.

Don't disconnect from your computer until your mp3 player says it's OK to disconnect, or you might damage the mp3's memory.

Need to write down some notes?

_____

_____

_____

_____

_____

_____

_____

_____

_____

Digital Cameras

Digital Cameras sure are fun!

I love the LCD view finder, how it shows the picture I just took, and how it previews pictures that are on the camera.

I love that you can bring your camera into a photo shop to have your digital pictures printed, or send them to a photo shop from your home computer, even print pictures at home with your printer.

I love that you can pick and choose which pictures you want to print! *No more printing the pictures that have my thumb halfway across the lens....*

On the next few pages, we'll talk about digital camera basics. Information you should know to get started, and get through those first frustrating moments...

Choosing a camera
When you are thinking about buying a digital camera, think about what you are going to use it for.

Digital Cameras, pixels

Will you carry it around with you?
Does it need it to be light and portable?
Are portraits important to you?
Does it have the features you want?

Often the first question a salesperson will ask you is:
"How much do you want to spend?"

Digital cameras range in price from about $100 to $500 and up. Besides the obvious bells and whistles, the main difference between them is "MegaPixels"!

What are MegaPixels
and why do you care what they are?

Simply put, they are the tiny dots that make up a digital picture. So, more dots = a clearer picture.

This might help you figure out what you need:

Camera's MegaPixels	Good quality pictures	Best quality pictures
4 - 5 MP	11 x 14"	5 x 7"
6 - 7 MP	16 x 20"	8 x 10"
8 MP	17 x 22"	8 x 10"
10 MP	20 X 30"	11 x 14"

Of course you can print smaller pictures! But, if you enlarge a picture that was taken with a 4MP camera to 16 x 20, the picture's going to be fuzzy.

Digital Cameras, memory

Storing pictures.

A digital camera, all by itself, generally holds about 24 pictures. But they can hold up to 800 pictures with the help of a "memory card".

Memory Cards

These are great little things that can hold a ton of pictures. Almost every digital camera has a small slot where you are supposed to insert a memory card. Think of it as extra rolls of film — only tiny and hardly thicker than a credit card!

What size of memory card do you need?
This chart shows approximately how many photos a card will hold with different sized cameras:

Camera Size	Photos on a 64MB card	Photos on a 128MB card	Photos on a 256MB card
4MP	40-50	90-100	170-190
5MP	35-40	70-80	140-160
6MP	25-30	55-65	110-125
8MP	20-25	35-40	75-80

Camera Size	Photos on a 512MB card	Photos on a 1GB card
4MP	360-400	725-800
5MP	280-315	560-625
6MP	225-250	450-500
8MP	150-165	300-330

Digital Cameras, transferring

Transferring..., Downloading...,
You can download images from your camera or from the memory card!

From your Camera to your Computer
You can download images to your computer in a couple of ways. One is with a USB cable that has one end specific to your camera. Plug one end into your camera, the other to your computer! Open your photo program and "import" the pictures.

Another way is via a "dock". Many digital cameras come with a dock option. The idea is that you leave the dock plugged into your computer so when you place the camera on it, it will open its program and download the pictures. Docks can also re-charge the camera's batteries!

Using a Memory Card Reader
Memory Card Readers are very handy, small devices. Remove the memory card from your camera and put it into the reader. Then insert the reader into a USB port on your computer. Open your photo program and import the pictures!

There.. Bob's your uncle!

Well, almost...

Digital Cameras, programs

Memory Card Readers
are small, connect to your
compuer via a USB port
and can read most types of
memory cards.

Viewing, Editing, Printing

Program choices...
Your digital camera most likely came with its own
photo program that will edit, delete, and do many
things with your pictures.

You don't have to use the program your camera came
with. There are many programs to choose from. But be
aware, not all photo programs are created equal!
Some programs are easier to use than others.

Some do fancier editing, some are so confusing you
wonder who on earth would ever use them!

Everyone will tell you their favorite.
Find one that works for you.

Digital Cameras, programs

Here are a few things to look for in a photo program:

Importing
Can the program detect and download pictures from your type of camera? From the memory card?

Exporting
Can the program easily communicate with your email program to email pictures?

Output abilities
Can the program save pictures in different types of files — condensed for emailing, high pixels for posters?

Online Albums
Does it offer an online photo gallery where you can share your pictures? For free? Or do you have to pay?

Editing
How easy is it to edit a picture? How many editing features does it have? If you like to Scrapbook, will it do what you want it to do?

Have a look at Windows Live Photo Gallery. It's a great basic program that's easy to use.

It comes with Windows 7 and can be downloaded if you use Vista or the 32 bit version of XP.

Digital Cameras, editing

All of a sudden you're a photo editor! Yikes!
Editing pictures can be the best part of having a digital camera, but it can also be the most confusing.
This quick explanation might make it easier for you.

To Edit a picture:

◊ You have to open a picture to edit it.

◊ You have to open an editing tool to activate it.

◊ The steps in using editing tools are generally the same. For instance:

   ◊ Open the picture.

   ◊ Choose the editing tool.

   ◊ Click over the picture or area of the picture you want to edit.

   ◊ Click to apply the edit.

◊ If you like the edit, SAVE it. If you want to keep the original, save the edited picture with a new name. Some programs like Windows Photo Gallery and iPhoto for Macs let you "revert" back to the original at any time!

THAT is a very condensed version of the truth!

Some editing tools require many steps and can be quite complicated. *See the next page for a glossary.*

When you are researching different types of image editing programs, check reviews for how good the program's "Help" sections are. Some programs have great step-by-step instructions... *Some, well, don't!*

Digital Cameras, editing

Photo Editing Tools: a Glossary

Crop
Choose what you want to keep in a photo and delete everything else.

Red Eye
This helps you remove red-eye.

Cloning
You can copy parts of a photo and paste it again and again onto another part of the photo.

Touch up
Can help you cover up things like pimples...wrinkles... The tool might work the same as Cloning.

Layers
Layers are cool. Think of a Layer as a clear sheet of glass over the photo. Create a layer, then add an effect. You don't actually change the image, only how you see it. You can add layers upon layers.

Transparency
Has to do with Layers, you can make a Layer more or less opaque by adjusting how *transparent* it is.

Layer Mask
A Mask is an object that you can put onto a Layer. You can then apply an effect to the area inside the area of the Mask and leave the rest of the layer clear.

Digital Cameras, editing

Photo Editing Tools: a Glossary

Light/Shadow Adjustment or Fill-flash
Corrects lighting problems. Maybe the background is too dark or the subject is too light - *or vice versa!*

Noise
If your picture looks grainy, usually the case when there is poor light, the grainy flecks are referred to as Noise.

Magic Wand
I love this tool! You can draw around an irregularly shaped object to either cut it out, copy the object or color it in. Play with this one!

Photo Fix Wizard
This is a nice feature some programs have. It walks you through the steps to edit or fix a picture.

Discover something? Write it down for next time!

Digital Cameras, emailing

To Email a Picture - *it's a snap!*

When you first use your photo program, make sure it is configured to work with the email program you use!

◊ Open your photo program and the folder (Album) with your pictures.

◊ Look for and open a tab that says Email, Send, Share, etc., something along that line!

◊ There should be an option where you can select the photos you want to send. You might have a choice of size. A smaller size is easier to send.

◊ Once your pictures are selected, look for a "send" or "email" button again. Then, either:

* A new email page will open with the pictures you have chosen attached to it, or

* Your pictures might be sent to an online album, with an email invitation sent to your friends to view them.

If your photo program does not do email...

Open your email and attach the pictures yourself!

You will have to "Browse" for the pictures you want to attach, so it is helpful to know where your photos are in your computer! *For example, maybe...*

My Documents / Kodak / Pictures / Date

Digital Cameras - Tips

Tip #1

When you download pictures, you will be asked, Do
you want to remove the images from your device?
Say YES, and the memory card and camera will
be emptied and ready use all over again. If you say
NO, you can still download into your computer, but
the pictures will stay on your camera, and card.

Tip #2

Eject before you disconnect! Before disconnecting a
camera or reader, be sure that your computer says it
is safe to disconnect.

Tip #3

Make sure your batteries are good to go! Carry new
ones! If your battery dies when you're "transferring"
images you COULD LOSE ALL your pictures!

Tip #4

Re-format = Erase! When a program asks, "Do you
want to reformat your memory disk?" if you re-format
a disk, you will erase any images on the disk.

Tip #5

To take the best quality pictures, use the largest
megapixel setting you can. For example, if you have
a 6MP camera, take pictures that are 6MP! You
can always reduce the megapixels for printing or
emailing, but you can't increase them.

Index

Index

Index

Find something else? Mark it down!

Learning computer basics, and beyond, can be easy.
With the *My Parents* series, it really is. Truly!

Sales from this and my other books help raise funds
for cancer research and patient care.

Let's find a cure.

Your comments and suggestions are always welcome.
Visit me at www.myparentsfirst.com
Or on Twitter @MyParentsTweet

Thank you to my husband, family and so
many friends who have helped me, in more ways
than I can say, with the writing of this book.

Literally yours, Louise

My Parents'
Computer Guide
~Beyond the Basics~

Live, Love, Learn

The sale of this book, and other books published by KLMK Enterprises, help to raise funds for cancer research and patient care. Find a cure.

Published by KLMK Enterprises
A small publishing house that knows no boundaries.
www.MyParentsFirst.com

ISBN 978-0-9732728-64
Printed by Hignell Printing, Winnipeg, MB Canada
April, 2010

My Parents' Computer Guide, Beyond the Basics

In this book I am assuming you already know the basics of how to use your computer — the basics found in *My Parents First Computer and Internet Guide.*

Windows 7, Vista and XP!

Between these covers you will find easy instructions for all three of these operating systems!

You'll learn the few simple steps it takes to do the regular maintenance on your computer to keep it running smoothly.

You'll have more fun with Word and get familiar with Excel.

We'll simplify using your cell phone, teach you how to text lightning fast and introduce you to Facebook, Twitter and Skype!

Life's good with today's technology.
But today's technology is a lot more fun when it's made easy to use!

My Parents' Computer Guide, Beyond the Basics

Customizing Your Computer

Revving Up Your Documents

SpreadSheet (Excel) Basics

My Parents' Computer Guide, Beyond the Basics

Internet Savvy

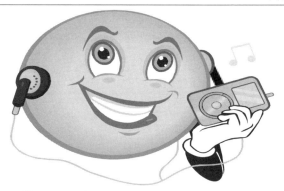

Beyond the Computer

Customize Your Computer

Setting up your computer
to work the way you want it to
is not only easy, but
doesn't take much time to do.

Customize Your Computer

GRAN

GW00635286

Contents

Written by Tony Kelly

Produced by Duncan Baird Publishing Limited, London, England
for AA Publishing
© Automobile Developments Limited 2002
Maps © Automobile Association Developments Limited 2002

Published in the United States by AAA Publishing,
1000 AAA Drive, Heathrow, Florida 32746
Published in the United Kingdom by AA Publishing

ISBN 1-56251-670-1

Color separation by Leo Reprographics
Printed and bound in China by Leo Paper Products

10 9 8 7 6 5 4 3 2 1